Into the Wind

Into the Wind

An Addict's Journey
toward Recovery

❧ ❧

by

Amanda Myers

❧ ❧

RedLine Books
White Bluff, Tennessee

ISBN 0-9727440-0-2

RedLine Books
2280 Jones Creek Rd.
White Bluff, Tennessee 37187
(615) 797 3043
bardy@bellsouth.net

Manufactured in the United States of America

This book is dedicated to all who find themselves captive to the disease of addiction. May you recover by seeing the light that shines within.

Introduction

On the morning of May 20, 1999, I received the news that my great-grandmother, Kathleen Angel, had died peacefully in her sleep. She died only two weeks before I entered treatment for an eating disorder. I began treatment still overwhelmed by memories of her smile, the way she smelled, how she hugged me when I entered her house.

In treatment, I was given many different tools for use in coping with difficult situations and uncomfortable emotions. The most therapeutic of these tools for me was writing. Writing meant total freedom. While my pen was on the paper, I was free from rules and regulations, free from time limits, free from anyone telling me I was right or wrong. The words on the paper were mine, and I could express myself without holding anything back.

During my time in treatment, I took an interest in poetry. I found something in poetry that I simply could not find in free writing or in keeping a journal. German poet Rainer Maria Rilke wrote, "Poetic power is great, strong as primitive instinct; it has its own unyielding rhythms in itself and breaks out as out of mountains" (56). Writing poetry led me to places in my mind that I had never visited. I was able to link people, places, and events that I had never associated before. One of the first poems I ever wrote describes my relationship with my great-grandmother. In writing this poem, I discovered that although she knew nothing of my eating disorder before her death, Mammaw Angel would be a vital part of my journey toward recovery.

I n t o   T h e   W i n d

I

She lives alone with her tv, always on.
Her life was once filled with activity—
cutting hair for everyone in town,
scolding my aunt for shaving her brother's hair
  with the electric razor left in the salon.
She once looked back to laugh.
Now, she simply waits and watches.

As I walk through the door she is filled:
face brightening, eyes widening, arms
  reaching out.
I hug her—not one of those delicate hugs,
  polite and full of fear for breaking an old woman,
but true and long—I do not let go first.
She has grown small, I taller.
She reaches up to cup my face and whispers,
  "My beautiful Amanda."

I wonder at what she sees.
She tells me I am beautiful,
that someday I'll find someone who
will cherish me for who I am,
will love me for being random and
  (laughing out loud)
will treasure me for strengths and weaknesses,
will love me as she loves me now . . .
  unconditionally.
I wish I could believe what she sees.

II

When the call comes, my mother answers.
Something inside the phone makes her droop, wilt.

Her eyes squinting against it, the tears spreading
  on her cheeks give the storm away.
"She died peacefully this morning,"
  she whispers.
Gravity is relentless on my heart.
Why now? Why today? Was God's need of her
  greater than my own?
Such questions serve only to teach acceptance.

I contemplate my time with her.
How many have time with great-grandparents?
How many remember them vividly?
I am a fortunate one; I have been blessed.
In my ears her words resound,
  "my beautiful Amanda,"
And someday I will believe them.

In a way, this poem represents my life; it illustrates my journey. I have spent so much time focusing on my defects and failures that I incessantly disregard any positive attributes I might have. Mine has been a journey toward acceptance of myself, my mistakes, and my accomplishments.

    I was unable to begin this journey, however, until I hit rock bottom. Dealing with and letting go of the pressure from the negative voices around me was the first step toward recovery. In her book titled *Dream Work*, Mary Oliver includes a poem called "The Journey," which, like my own poem, addresses my situation. It is an accurate and eloquent representation of what I had to do in order to heal:

One day you finally knew
what you had to do, and began,
though the voices around you
kept shouting

their bad advice—
though the whole house
began to tremble
and you felt the old tug
at your ankles.
"Mend my life!"
each voice cried.
But you didn't stop.
You knew what you had to do,
though the wind pried
with its stiff fingers
at the very foundations—
though their melancholy
was terrible.
It was already late
enough, and a wild night,
and the road full of fallen
branches and stones.
But little by little,
as you left their voices behind,
the stars began to burn
through the sheets of clouds,
and there was a new voice,
which you slowly
recognized as your own,
that kept you company
as you strode deeper and deeper
into the world,
determined to do
the only thing you could do—
determined to save
the only life you could save. (114-15)

Introduction

One of the first lessons I learned in treatment is that I am responsible only for myself. My life is the only life I can save. This lesson is true for all—but especially for those of us who abuse or are addicted to various substances such as alcohol, food, or drugs. It is not until we are accountable for our own actions that we can begin the journey toward an addiction-free lifestyle. Recovery is a strenuous but rewarding journey shared only by those addicts willing to follow a different path and face the consequences of their actions.

The next three of the following chapters are devoted to the preliminary research for a larger creative project based on my own personal story of recovery and forms the last chapter of this book, which I call "Treasures of Strength and Weakness." Along with the story of my own recovery from anorexia and bulimia, I have included the stories of three other addicts in chapter 3: Diane, Jim, and Molly. The fact that all three of them are recovering alcoholics, not individuals who suffered specifically from eating disorders, is, as I hope to make clear, irrelevant. Addiction is addiction. I have changed the names of my three friends to maintain anonymity and honor confidentiality. These four stories, theirs and my own, make clear that although each addict is on a separate journey the paths parallel one another and, at various times, intersect, for a variety of reasons. The individuals in the following stories are bound by the feelings of fear, anger, and denial that once ruled their lives. Whether life is viewed as a journey or as the sum of many small journeys, the net result is the same: the journey is a challenge requiring awareness, acceptance, and commitment. My intention in sharing these stories is to reveal the bonds shared by all addicts and to show that the principles of recovery can be applied to any journey in life.

Less than a year after I began my journey of recovery, I embarked on yet another unique journey. Along with fifteen others, I pedaled my bicycle the 445 miles from Maryville, Tennessee, to Savannah, Georgia. Just like each stage of my recovery, each mile brought new challenges to meet and obstacles to overcome. The parallels between my recovery and the bike trip are intriguing. Consequently, the bike trip will be the basis, the controlling metaphor, of my novella. My plan is to write in the present tense about both my bike trip and my time in treatment. I will also include the journeys of Diane, Jim, and Molly as inspiration and reminders of strength and hope. Each story will foster and draw upon the ideas and themes in the others.

Still, until I have accumulated all of the information for the final story, a number of questions will remain unanswered about the structure and content of the final product. One year ago I would have been intimidated by the unanswered questions and lack of rigid structure that accompany this stage of my project. Today, however, I am reminded of the words of Rainer Maria Rilke:

> [B]e patient toward all that is unsolved in your heart and try to love the questions themselves like locked rooms and like books that are written in a very foreign tongue. Do not now seek the answers which cannot be given you because you would not be able to live them. And the point is, to live everything. Live the questions now. . . . [P]erhaps you will then, gradually, without noticing it, live along some distant day into the answers. (79)

Into the Wind

Planting a Seed

Better to light one candle than to curse the darkness.

— *Chinese Proverb*

Imagine a disease that spreads through the nation like wildfire taking the lives of America's most talented and ambitious young men. Imagine an epidemic that slowly kills America's football stars, its top medical students, and its aspiring young male celebrities by turning them away from food or compelling them to rid their bodies of all nourishment through self-induced vomiting. In her book *The Beauty Myth* (Perennial, 2002), Naomi Wolf concludes that a disease ravaging America's "favorite sons" would receive immediate attention: "crisis task forces convened in congressional hearing rooms, unscheduled alumni meetings, the best experts money can hire, cover stories in news magazines, a flurry of editorials, blame and counterblame, bulletins, warnings, symptoms, updates; an epidemic blazoned in boldface red" (180). This disease is real. But it afflicts our girls, and it is quiet, and it is secretive, and America does not want to deal with it because it does not fix easily.

W. R. Spence, M.D., author of the pamphlet "Eating Disorders: Starving for Perfection," claims that "at least 3 million people have some form of eating disorder. Seventy percent of women in the United States believe themselves to be overweight; and 15–20 percent of eating-disorder victims die from their disease" (4). Despite these startling statistics, American society continues to idealize thinness and place a tremendous amount of pressure on women "to validate their self-worth, and please others, by controlling their appearance" (Moorey, 41). This epidemic is not limited to the United States. In her essay "Eating Disorders: The History of Body Image," Nancy Davis states that "The Duchess of Windsor is reported to have said, 'No woman can be too rich or too thin'—a powerful illustration of our cultural obsession with the impossible ideal." Moorey also asserts that a thin body has become a "symbol of success, beauty, competence, and worth" (41). Cultural standards and the influence of mass media are important contributors to eating disorders, exceeded in importance only by a family history of addictions and family overemphasis on achievement and perfection (Spence, 4). Although studies have proven the negative effects of the media's emphasis on a small body size, few changes have taken place, and eating disorders continue as a silent killer of young women.

Medical professionals have struggled for centuries to classify anorexia and bulimia. Arguments continue to arise regarding the specific nature and precise descriptions of these eating disorders. Anorexia nervosa has been classified in categories ranging from psychiatric disorder to physical illness, and it "has even been dismissed as non-existent" (Moorey, 15). Undeniably, both disorders are complex and potentially fatal medical situations. Still, there is no universally accepted definition of either anorexia or bulimia. Clinical psychologist Richard A. Gordon defines anorexia and bulimia as "disorders of development that revolve around the core issues of shape and body weight, and in which the person, typically female, obsessively focuses on the achievement of thinness in order to solve problems of personal identity" (30). Anorexia, often more fully identified as anorexia nervosa, is anchored in a compulsive avoidance of food stimulated by a pathological fear of gaining weight. The word *anorexia* literally means *without appetite*. Bulimia, literally *great hunger,* is an equally serious disorder and the opposite side of the same dreadful coin. The bulimic is compulsively driven to overeat and then to purge, that is, to vomit the undigested food. Thus the two disorders are often tied together in one personality: compulsive avoidance of food followed by dangerous overeating, purging, and so on. For anyone outside the mind of the sufferer, nothing about this behavior makes any sense. For the anorexic-bulimic caught in the grip of the disease, nothing else matters.

Young people between the ages of twelve and twenty-five are the most vulnerable candidates for anorexia and bulimia, and college campuses tend to be the most common environment for the development of eating disorders (Gordon 47). In addition to a predisposition to the disease because of age, college life exaggerates factors that increase a person's chance of developing an eating disorder. Richard Gordon specifies these factors as "a fluid and unstructured environment, social and academic competition, a concern with appearance and physical attractiveness, and a destructured eating environment in which food binging and weight gain are commonplace" (47). Comfort can be found in knowing that some colleges have started programs specifically geared toward helping students who suffer from eating disorders. Unfortunately, however, anorexia continues to affect up to 25 percent of female college students, bulimia up to 19 percent, and studies have shown that vast numbers of students, male and female, eat uncontrollably for a variety of reasons (Hesse-Biber, 89–90).

If I had been familiar with these statistics before I left home for college, perhaps they could have alerted me to a problem I did not identify until I had paid an enormous price. When I was a sophomore in college, a member of the varsity volleyball team, and a straight-A student, I was perceived by my peers and even some of my professors as "the girl who's got it all under control." I had established a reputation of such stability that no one even suspected that I might have a problem.

In reality I fell into the category with so many other girls my age; I was among the 25 percent of college women with anorexia and the 19 percent of college women who suffer from bulimia. Richard Gordon states that "underneath a facade of good behavior, they [anorexics] typically feel weak, unworthy, and obligated to live up to what they perceive as being relentless demands for perfection" (16). The same concept seems to hold true for bulimics as well. Gordon comments that a bulimic upholds a positive facade on the surface. Underneath, however, the bulimic "feels needy, childlike, dependent, feelings of which she is deeply ashamed. Under no circumstances does she permit herself to reveal her primitive feelings of abandonment, sadness, and rage" (60–61). I had created a facade so impervious that not even I knew "the real me."

In health and psychology classes throughout both high school and college, I had learned the basic definition of eating disorders. Still, I had never known or read about anyone who really suffered from anorexia or bulimia. For this reason I want to use my story as the basis of this book. My hope is that it will provide knowledge useful to young people, especially college-age students, who are vulnerable to or who suffer from this deadly disease or who might know someone who is suffering from it and recognize the symptoms. I want to displace ignorance with insight so that all of us can become part of someone's solution and not part of the problem. I do not expect that my story will cause any sort of epiphany in the anorexic or bulimic who reads it. My goal, however, is simply to plant a seed of hope. I want to say pointedly to those suffering from eating disorders that there is a way out of the vicious cycles that dominate the lives of anorexics and bulimics. I want to provide those in similar situations something that

I did not have when I was feeling worthless, hopeless, and suicidal. I want to show them the path to recovery from the perspective of someone on the journey, to assert that there is a life full of happiness and freedom beyond the chains of this disease.

Although my main goal is to share my experience, strength, and hope with those still suffering from anorexia and bulimia, I have also found working on this book to be therapeutic and beneficial to my own recovery. In a recovery meeting, I was told that I should maintain my anonymity, unless betraying it would benefit my own recovery. I look at the writing of this book as part of my healing process. Still, this kind of writing is accompanied by fear and anxiety because it requires that I think and speak to a large audience about the issues that I have found so damaging in my private life. My biggest fear in writing my story is expressed most eloquently in a poem called "The Invitation," by Oriah Mountain Dreamer. In the poem, she writes,

> It doesn't interest me if the story you're telling me is true,
> I want to know if you can disappoint another to be true to
>   yourself;
> If you can bear the accusation of betrayal and not betray your
>   own soul.

My disease and recovery involve both positive and negative actions of my family, my friends, my doctors, and myself. I risk not only betraying myself, but others. Still, the success of this project is dependent upon my risk in being true to my feelings and myself—a task that might upset those who are dear to me. Despite this fear, I eagerly anticipate the healing and closure that can develop from this writing (ad)venture.

Establishing Roots

It's my life; it's better left to chance. I could have missed the pain, but I'd have had to miss the dance.

— *Garth Brooks*

I have only vague memories of my sophomore year of college. I was so obsessed with food, weight, and body image that I neglected every other aspect of my life. I planned every minute of my day around how many calories I ate and the location of the nearest one-person bathroom. In other words, anorexia and bulimia consumed my mind and dictated my actions. Only in retrospect, however, have I come to recognize the power of this disease and its impact on my life. Although

I can remember specific incidents, the vast majority of my sophomore year is a blur. Therefore, I have had to rely heavily on the memories of those people who took care of me, stood by me, and eventually coerced me into treatment for my eating disorders.

In August 1998, I returned to Maryville College after spending my entire summer at a local church camp as a counselor. Being a camp counselor was one of the most rewarding experiences of my life. Activities such as rock climbing, repelling, and intense ropes courses taught me how much I like to push my limits and stretch my comfort zone. While at camp, however, I began to have extreme stomach pains after every meal. To avoid the pain, I simply decreased the amount of food I ate at each meal. It seemed logical, and my stomach pains decreased. The combination of decreased food intake and constant activity inevitably led to weight loss. I was thrilled by the fact that I was losing weight. So I continued to lessen my food intake while justifying my actions with the pains that resulted from a full stomach.

On returning to school for volleyball preseason training, my roommate, Melanie, noticed a change in my eating patterns; however, she attributed this change to the summer at camp and the fact that I told her I had become a vegetarian. As volleyball season progressed, I found it more difficult to function on such small amounts of food. While babysitting one night, the strawberries I had eaten for dinner irritated my stomach to the point that I felt nauseated. Without a second thought, I went to the bathroom, stuck my fingers down my throat, and threw up everything I had eaten. Although I had never experimented with drugs, I must assume that the feeling was much like that of getting high. I was able to eat, purge, and still remain in control of my weight. In short, I was hooked. From this point on, I would eat small meals, such as a bowl of cereal or a bagel, and I would immediately go to the bathroom and throw up.

The stomach pains never completely subsided, and the athletic trainers sent me to a gastroenterologist, who diagnosed me with a spastic colon. Because the doctor never asked about my eating habits or suspected an eating disorder, I immediately realized how easily I could hide my behavior and what I later found to be a deadly disease.

For the next few months I was able to hide the fact that I was purging all of my food, and I hid my weight loss by wearing baggy clothing. Melanie, however, was determined to get me out of the baggy clothes and into tight, revealing outfits to impress my boyfriend. Although she was simply trying to help me, I took her actions to mean, "You don't look good enough." Naturally, this augmented my feelings of unworthiness and sent me deeper into my eating disorder. I became so ashamed of my body that I could not let my boyfriend get too close to me without pulling away. I did not want him to see what I often described as the body of a "water-retaining sea cow."

Malnutrition quickly led to brain starvation, and I lost my ability to think clearly and make decisions. I also suffered from temporary memory loss. Only with the help of my roommate, my counselor, and a close friend have I been able to reconstruct the events leading up to my admittance into the hospital for anorexia and bulimia.

By late November 1998 I was constantly battling strep throat, which required long-term antibiotics. Therefore, I was unable to participate in the post-finals festivities. I went to a party, however, and watched as everyone, including Melanie, drank *Jack Daniels* and *José Cuervo*. At the end of the night, Melanie was so intoxicated that self-induced vomiting was the only way to avoid a terrible hangover. Trying to be a good friend, I explained to Melanie that throwing up was easy. "All you have to do," I said, "is stick your finger down your throat until you hit your gag reflex. Trust me, I'm an expert at this." She looked at me with a puzzled expression but was too drunk to say more than "We'll talk about this tomorrow." To this day I am not sure why I divulged my secret: perhaps I simply could not keep a secret any longer; perhaps I acted out of fear of the encroaching sickness; perhaps my moment of openness was a cry for help. No matter what rationale I use for my comment that evening, it was the beginning of a long and arduous journey.

Three weeks later, I had lost at least ten more pounds, and I was becoming considerably weaker and less coherent. My roommate became even more concerned when I almost ran a red light despite the four people in my car yelling at me to stop. Melanie said, "It was like you couldn't even hear us." Later that day, Melanie ran into my ex-boyfriend, who asked how I was doing. Being so worried about me, she broke down and told him that she thought I had an eating disorder. He immediately recalled how little I had eaten over the months we had dated, and he decided that he and Melanie should confront me.

The following day Melanie and Chad spent hours on the Internet looking up information about eating disorders. Melanie later explained to me: "Everything about you came together. Your perfectionism, your fear of being alone, your total physical appearance, such as hair loss, pale, dry skin, and weight loss, all warning signs of someone with an eating disorder." That night, after Melanie and Chad had concluded their Internet research, I was lying in bed and was startled when Melanie walked in and blurted, "We have to talk."

I was so paranoid at that point that my response was, "What have I done now?" She told me that she felt that I had a serious problem with eating. After hours of talking and crying in the dark, I told Melanie everything about my eating habits. I begged her not to tell anyone, and she agreed as long as I would try to eat. I told her that I would do whatever she asked as long as she kept quiet. Thus, we had a plan; we were going to beat this "thing" together.

Her first request as "nurse Melanie" was that I drink Pedialyte, a nutrient-rich drink for babies, in order to restore some of the nutrients my body desperately needed. Each time she filled a cup with Pedialyte, it took at least an hour for me to finish it. I do remember the excruciating pain I felt every time I had any type of food or drink in my body. Eventually, I reached the point that my body automatically rejected the Pedialyte, and I purged it out of my system. Our attempt to conquer this disease by ourselves lasted only two or three days.

I continued all of my regular activities, such as going to classes and working out for volleyball, in order to maintain the facade that I was fine. Like most volleyball players, I work out in spandex shorts and a T-shirt. Apparently, my clothing made it evident that I was sick. One of the student trainers, who was also one of my teammates, confronted Melanie in the weight room and said, "Amanda is sick, isn't she? As a student trainer, it's my responsibility to report anything suspicious concerning Maryville College athletes to the head trainers." Knowing it was the right thing to do, Melanie did not stop the student trainer from divulging my secret. The head trainer asked to meet with me, and she gave me the phone number of a local therapist named Peggy. I called and made an appointment, but I was still unable to keep any food in my body.

Before I could meet with Peggy, I became so weak that Melanie decided that I needed to tell my closest friends, who were constantly asking what was wrong with me; she also made the decision to take me to the school nurse, Cydna. At 8 o'clock the following morning, Melanie and Leah escorted me to the health clinic. Reluctantly, I entered Cydna's office while my friends waited in the lobby. I tried to be dismissive, nonchalantly stating that my friends thought I had an eating disorder, but Cydna remembers that it was obvious something was wrong; I was slumping in the chair, I looked extremely fatigued, and I made no eye contact. She asked about my medical history and gathered as many details regarding my eating habits as I would disclose.

Eventually, Cydna called the girls into her office and ordered them to take me directly to the emergency room. In addition to the countless tests I endured while at the hospital, I went through my first addiction assessment for eating disorders. The addiction counselor from the Southeast Recovery Center asked me pages of questions about my family history and my personal battle with food. She explained to me the severity of the disease and requested that I return the following week to enter treatment; I rudely explained that I did not need to be in a treatment center for anything, picked up my things, and staggered out the door. I felt such hostility toward that woman that I sarcastically gave her the title "my BFF (best friend forever) Judy Hayes."

The hospital sent my blood tests to Cydna at the health clinic. At this point, Cydna knew I could not face the cure alone. She also attempted to explain the severity of my condition. She added that although it would be hard, I could overcome this disease.

I finally met with Peggy, who has been my therapist for more than a year. Of those first few months, Peggy recalls:

> I couldn't get over how much you did, how much you were involved in, and how much you didn't know what was going on with you. I kept thinking, how are we going to slow this down enough to get you to take a look at what was happening? My overall impression of you early on was that you were fast, you did *not* want to accept that something was really wrong, and that you were going to have to change your lifestyle in some way. There were many times I wondered how sick would your whole life get before you were willing to change?

To the dismay of both my counselor and my friends, my condition progressively worsened. Melanie recalls that I ate only rice cakes and still proceeded to the bathroom after every meal. In addition to the fact that I refused to eat more than rice cakes, I was so depressed that

I became self-destructive. In retrospect, it seems that I had become so numb to everything around me that I was searching for ways to feel pain. Melanie soon began hiding any objects that I might use to hurt myself.

I finally decided that I just wanted to go to sleep for a long time and avoid everything that made my life miserable. Late one night after Melanie was asleep, I took an entire bottle of muscle relaxers left over from an athletic injury. All that I remember is waking up the next morning extremely angry that my plan had failed. Realizing that I was in a precarious situation, I went to Cydna's office and confessed the events of the previous evening. Once again I found myself in the hospital undergoing tests and another addiction assessment with "my BFF Judy Hayes." After answering questions for over an hour, I was told that I needed to consider partial hospitalization for treatment of anorexia, bulimia, and a suicide attempt, which would require me to withdraw from school. I vaguely remember thanking them for their concern and explaining that under no circumstances would I quit school to go into the hospital. It would be another two months before I went back to the hospital.

I relied heavily on the support and guidance of Peggy, Cydna, and a select group of friends and professors; however, I constantly worried about abusing their friendships; so I would isolate myself from everyone for days at a time. Still, my condition continued to deteriorate. By the end of the year, I was finally beginning to recognize the severity of my disease. Each morning I found more bald spots where my hair had fallen out during the night; my skin was dry, scaly, and covered with acne; I suffered from amenorrhea, the absence of menstrual periods. Something had to be done.

Fearing for my life, Peggy and Cydna convinced me that I really needed to use the summer to focus on getting better. After researching treatment centers all over the nation, I reluctantly went to Southeast Recovery Center. There I would undergo my third assessment in less than six months. Luckily, this assessment was conducted by a new lady, Christy, who made me feel more comfortable than "my BFF Judy Hayes." On June 8, 1999, I was hospitalized in the Southeast Recovery Center to undergo treatment for anorexia and bulimia. The fear I experienced stepping off the elevator on that first day is not easily compared to anything I have ever endured. The fear of the unknown, of dealing with my problems, of giving up my eating disorder was almost enough to make me turn around and go home. But the greater fear of letting down Peggy and Cynda prevailed, and I walked into the waiting room and signed my name on the clipboard for the first time. I spent the first three hours signing forms. The man who conducted my orientation said, "The basis of our program is abstinence; we ask that you not purge while you are here."

My only thought was *Hell, if I could do that, I wouldn't be here!* During my lunch break, which I did not use to eat lunch, I called both Peggy and Cydna, crying. I begged for permission to leave; I was not supposed to be in the hospital. I was not like those other people; I still weighed over one hundred pounds and therefore refused to accept that I really had an eating disorder. To my mind, people with eating disorders weighed under a hundred pounds, and that figure did not apply to me.

For three weeks, I spoke only when I was addressed directly, I was uncooperative, and I never smiled. I learned later that patients suffering from eating disorders are even more difficult to treat than alcoholics or drug addicts. They find opening up and relinquishing what they perceive as control almost impossible. I spent my mornings with doctors and nurses, who made sure that I was not losing more weight and that my heart and other organs were still functioning properly. Most afternoons were spent in group therapy, art therapy, or educational sessions. One afternoon, however, all of the patients were loaded into a van and taken for an outing in the mountains. Cramped in the back of the vehicle between a drug addict whose body was covered with body piercings and tattoos, some of which were misspelled, and a woman who was still shaking from alcohol withdrawal, I was filled with hatred for everyone who thought I should be in treatment. I was not like these people, and I stubbornly committed to separating myself from them.

Although I did not speak during therapy sessions, I could not help listening to the stories "those people" told. The guy with the tattoos turned out to be the oldest of four children, just like me. His parents expected nothing less than excellence from him, and for most of his life he complied. Finally, the stress of being a perfectionist became too great, and he turned to drugs as an escape. Drugs took him away from the demands of family, school, and life in general.

The woman suffering from withdrawal had been caught in the middle of her parents' failing marriage for most of her life. Her mother vented frustrations concerning her father, while the father relentlessly bombarded her with the sad details of the marriage. The woman turned to alcohol as an escape, and her habit quickly moved beyond her control.

Three weeks into treatment I realized that I, too, had turned to something, the abuse of food, for escape. By controlling my food intake, I felt in control of my life. I found that as I opened up and accepted as my own the many similarities shared among all of the people within the rooms of the treatment center, I began to make it through the days, one at a time, without purging. Still, I experienced the withdrawal from purging much like an alcoholic or addict experiences a withdrawal from alcohol or drugs. My desire to purge was so strong that the effort to resist heading for the bathroom often reduced me to the fetal position, on the floor.

As the pains of withdrawal became less severe, I learned to identify and deal with the triggers, which are the foods, people, places, and feelings that caused me to purge. I was educated about the importance of following the food-guide pyramid and of accepting food as necessary fuel for my body. Most importantly, I learned to identify the variety of feelings associated with my disease. One of the counselors taught me that "no matter how the eating disorder manifests itself, there is a lot of self-hatred, self-loathing, and self-punishment being acted out." I was punishing myself for not being perfect in every aspect of my life.

By the end of my fourth week in the hospital, I had opened up to the group and accepted them as friends. I slowly learned to let down the wall I had built around myself. I found joy in a world that I had believed to be full of misery. I even learned that "my BFF Judy Hayes" was one of the most caring people on the unit. I looked forward to my time at the hospital because it filled me with strength and hope. Most importantly, I learned to smile. I soon found that I was leading the groups. One of the men in the therapy sessions told me, "Amanda, you're the backbone of this group; we draw a lot of strength from you." For the first time in over a year, I felt that my life was worthwhile.

After seven weeks in the hospital, I graduated from the Southeast Recovery Center. I remember every moment of that day. Peggy, Cydna, and all of my counselors and friends from the hospital were at the ceremony. The day was filled with congratulations, hugs, laughter, and tears. I was finally getting better. I left the hospital healthier and happier than I had been in over a year.

Like every other aspect of my life, I planned to work a perfect recovery program. I returned to school expecting to participate in all of the same activities while working a perfect program. This lasted for only a few weeks. I quickly found that I was no longer focusing on my recovery; I quit practicing the things I had learned in treatment; I thought that I was completely healed. On Labor Day 1999 I relapsed.

For three months, I went back and forth between my disease and my recovery. Peggy became worried and suggested that I consider returning to treatment. On November 28, 1999, however, I received the most wonderful gift. A dear friend gave me a *Recovery Bible,* which is full of recovery-based meditations. By making a commitment to work in the Bible for at least fifteen minutes every day, I have enhanced my spiritual life and sustained a steady recovery. Still, I have learned that I cannot work a perfect program; I am human. When I neglect my recovery for even a moment, I enter dangerous territory. If I leave out my daily prayers and Bible study, and if I begin isolating myself from my support group, I can be sure that my recovery will suffer.

Here's the bottom line: I must work every day to maintain my "sobriety." Some days are more difficult than others; however, I have learned to deal with the bad days in new and better ways. Cydna told me, "Amanda, you are clearer now than you were back then. You've been through treatment; you have the tools at hand to know where to go and what to do if you choose." From now on, I must choose to live or to die, choose to do or be undone, choose to fight or to surrender. Peggy once told me that every person is given a chance at life, a chance to dance. Today, I choose to dance.

Branching Out

I am a part of all that I have met.
— *Alfred, Lord Tennyson*

It is often challenging for non-addicts to see how alcoholism, drug addictions, and eating disorders are related. All three are diseases of addiction; the difference lies in the "drug of choice." Whether their stories or mine, a common thread binds all of us—we are addicts. Throughout my recovery, I have learned as much from alcoholics and drug addicts as I have from bulimics and anorexics. Although each addict has a unique journey, themes such as denial, anger, fear, perfection, failure, and success can be found along each path. What follows are the accounts of three recovering alcoholics whose stories, though distinct in their own ways, share a common thread not only with one another but with my experience in a recovery. I might have chosen the story of a recovering cocaine or heroin addict, and that story, too, would have connected to my own story of addiction. What is crucial to understand in all these stories is that the common threads of addiction, acceptance, and commitment weave all these stories together.

Diane Richards

Diane Richards began drinking at the age of 13. She began out of curiosity and with the added incentive of peer pressure, and she did it only sporadically, so drinking was never a serious problem. Diane married when she was eighteen years old. By the time she was twenty-five, she and her husband kept alcohol in the house, but they never drank in front of their children. As eight-year members of a civic organization, Diane and her husband went to many parties; it was during this time that Diane learned how to be "a good drunk." She could out-drink anyone, including the men, and she quickly became overtly proud of this fact.

Around the age of thirty-five, Diane crossed the line dividing a social drinker from an alcoholic. In 1992 Diane mentioned to her husband that she thought she might be an alcoholic. He denied that possibility, convinced her otherwise, and the drinking continued. By 1993 Diane's entire life revolved around alcohol. She admits to fixing a drink as soon as she got out of bed "to get over the withdrawals." In retrospect Diane realizes that alcohol was always around the house and that she was always thinking about it.

Problems began to arise as the result of Diane's alcohol abuse. She embarrassed her children, she was in financial trouble because she simply "let bills go," and she found herself crying all of the time. "I thought I was crazy, but I denied any problem with alcohol."

Sometimes the most unusual circumstances lead addicts toward the path to recovery. Diane entered treatment for the first time in January 1993. Her mother escorted her to the treatment floor of the hospital. As soon as she arrived, she decided that she did not want to be there, and she left. Walking through the parking lot, however, Diane heard her name being called. She turned around to find a very large nurse chasing after her. The nurse, out of breath and clasping her chest, called to Diane, "You know you need to be here."

"Yes, I do," Diane agreed, "but I'm not staying today."

Convincingly, the nurse retorted, "You may not be alive to come back. I ran all the way down here to get you and my titties hurt."

This explanation was good enough for Diane, and she turned to her mother and said, "Well, if her titties hurt, I guess I should go back up there." During her two-week stay in the hospital, Diane found out that she was the only person that nurse had ever chased. Despite the comedy of the situation, Diane credits that nurse with opening the doors leading to the path of recovery.

Diane has been through many different treatment centers in the past seven years. At first she could not stop looking at the differences between her and the other addicts. When she finally realized the tie that binds her to others suffering from diseases of addiction, she was able to learn more about her disease and its power. "Unfortunately," she recalls, "I was always in treatment for the wrong reasons; I did it to save my job or please my family. I didn't understand how hard you have to work at it, and I never took the warnings about relapse to heart."

Learning means nothing if a person simply stores the knowledge and never uses it. Diane was constantly learning the importance of setting boundaries, making lifestyle changes, and being self-aware. Instead of using this knowledge, however, she placed it in the back of her mind, despite the warnings from her friends in recovery that "unless you apply what you learn, you will drink again." In other words, if an addict does not make changes, if he does not try to do things differently, he will relapse. Diane refused to make changes in her life, and she relapsed. Still, the severity of her disease and the signals pointing to its seriousness did not get through to Diane, and she went back and forth between relapse and sobriety for many years.

In January 2000 Diane became so despondent that she decided the world would be better off without her. She took twenty-six prescription sleeping pills, consumed large quantities of vodka, and lay down on her couch to die. When the ambulance arrived with her mother and boyfriend, Diane was unconscious. After an extended stay in the hospital, Diane finally accepted the need for the changes she had to make in her life. This time, she vowed to get sober instead of saying, "I am going to try to get sober." She made a daily commitment to her recovery. She attends weekly recovery meetings, reads recovery literature, and prays to her higher power. Any time she finds herself withdrawing from others in recovery, avoiding meetings, and skipping her daily devotions, Diane can be sure that a relapse is in the future unless she changes her behavior.

Jim Walker

Jim Walker is not the typical "down-in-the-dirt alcoholic." Despite his alcoholism, he was able to maintain an upper-middle-class lifestyle, a good job, and a successful second marriage. Eventually, however, Jim was forced to admit his addiction to alcohol when his wife caught him sneaking drinks after promising that he had stopped and when his deteriorating health forced him time and again into hospitalization.

Jim took his first "real" drink of alcohol while attending a college thousands of miles from home in 1960s California. In Jim's account the new influences in his life, "dorm-life, frat parties, and post-game hysteria," were instrumental in establishing the drinking habits that would eventually lead him into a treatment center for alcoholism. His first job after graduation from college sent him traveling around the country; the company paid for all expenses—no questions asked. Thus, Jim drank with his clients and developed a high tolerance for alcohol in any form. Jim remembers, "I never passed out, never got stopped while driving, and never did anything to compromise society. When I moved to Europe, I realized that Europeans saw drinking as socially acceptable. So, I became socially acceptable—I drank."

While in his thirties, Jim was away on business at least fifty weeks a year, which he justified by being the breadwinner of the family. He spent these fifty weeks living in hotels, entertaining clients, and taking care of those who could not hold their liquor: "They were the ones with the problem. I could hold my alcohol." While traveling strengthened Jim's drinking habit, it weakened and eventually destroyed his marriage. He and his wife divorced, and Jim found even more time for traveling and drinking. Still, he came home on alternate weekends to spend time with his only son.

Tragically, Jim's son died after being hit head-on by a drunk driver. Naturally, this traumatic event altered Jim's habit. Sadly, however, it did not root out the problem. Instead, Jim changed the way he drank: "I swore that I would never again be behind the wheel of a car while I was drinking; so, I switched from being an open drinker to one in hiding. Instead of drinking with my clients, I would have water or tea and then retire to my room and drink until I passed out."

Eventually, Jim remarried, but he did not allow this change to affect his drinking. Soon, Jim developed acute pancreatitis, kidney problems, and liver damage. Because he showed no outward signs related to alcoholism, he was able to convince the doctors and his wife that he was not drinking. Looking back, Jim remembers, "Deep down, I knew something was wrong, but I didn't want to admit it.

Business was great, and I continued to do things that no one else could do."

He quickly learned, however, how to use the pancreatitis to his advantage. He knew exactly how much to drink in order to be put into the hospital and get some time off from work. When he began to show outward symptoms of alcoholism, such as hand tremors, hangovers, slacking on the job, and spending days at a time in bed, Jim's wife ordered him to seek help. Even though he agreed to see a doctor, he told his wife that he was not drinking at all and continued to deny any problems related to alcohol.

Finally, in December 1998, Jim's second wife caught him sneaking a drink from his suitcase while they were on vacation. She immediately left, which left Jim with two major realizations:

> First, I realized that I was losing a person that I loved very much and was causing her to stop loving me; and second, I was killing myself. Finally, it sunk in, and everything everybody had been telling me, everything that I had been denying, everything that I had ignored the existence of came as a stark, cold slap in the face: I was killing myself drinking and I was going to lose everything that meant anything at all to me.

Two days later Jim Walker checked himself into a treatment center where he spent six weeks learning the nature of his disease. Like Diane and me, Jim suffered from the "I'm-not-like-them syndrome." It took a long time before he could look beyond the differences between him and the other addicts. Jim confesses, "When I finally accepted that I am an alcoholic, I was able to see that I *am* like them." Accepting this relationship, Jim was able to learn from others who suffer from alcoholism.

At this writing it has been a year of sobriety for Jim, full of acceptance and of understanding for what addicts must face. He no longer has to plan vacations around the possibility of his alcohol being confiscated in the airport or the location of the nearest liquor store. He has also learned that no matter how much he does not want to attend a recovery meeting, he must go in order to maintain his sobriety. He reminds himself that "there is something in every meeting that makes it a worthwhile meeting. That something can keep an addict sober for today." He has learned that today is all we can concern ourselves with because it may be all we have.

Molly Jones

On March 17, 2000, Molly Jones celebrated thirteen years of sobriety. Molly, however, is an atypical recovering alcoholic in that she has never been through treatment. Instead, Molly credits Alcoholics Anonymous (AA) and other recovering alcoholics with giving her a second chance at life. She was fortunate to be among the 25 percent of people who come into the AA program and are able to maintain sobriety. Despite the low statistics, the AA recovery program is the most effective means of recovery.

Growing up, Molly was under constant pressure to produce high-quality work. As she sees it, "Rebellion was inevitable." Being the awkward kid with glasses and the daughter of the school principal, Molly's young life was characterized by ridicule. She quickly developed feelings of worthlessness, and she used alcohol to escape those feelings. By the age of twenty-four, Molly realized that she had a problem with alcohol. "I wished so badly that I could stop," she remembers, "but I had no control." For at least ten years, Molly tried to stop on her own through church, journaling, drinking only on the weekends, and repeatedly checking out the Alcoholics Anonymous *Big Book* from the public library; none of these approaches gave her what she needed to stop drinking.

After a day of drinking at the lake, Molly returned home to finish a report for work. Sitting on the floor, completely intoxicated, Molly realized that she could not go on living such a miserable existence. She needed some source outside herself for guidance and answers. She knew of the existence of Alcoholics Anonymous, and she managed to call the AA hotline. Like other addicts, she expressed herself to the AA representative as someone "who has a friend who has a drinking problem and needs to know where the nearest AA meeting is located." She now finds it funny that she had to call the police department to get directions to the AA meeting location.

She arrived at the meeting still drunk and scared to death. Molly's first memory of this meeting is of a lady reaching across the table and telling her, "You don't have to do this alone anymore." She attended five consecutive days of these meetings and then decided to attempt recovery on her own; this lasted for only another five days. Molly spent the next month in a drunken haze until she experienced what she labels "divine intervention." Part of her job included driving advertising clients around town. By the grace of God, Molly ended up in a car for seven hours with a man who had been sober for three years and could not stop talking about AA.

Molly quickly found herself back in AA meetings. Her first return meeting stands out as one of the most profound experiences of her life. She remembers:

> As we stood there holding hands at the end of the meeting saying the Lord's Prayer, I felt a presence, I felt a peace, I felt the desire to drink lifted out of me. It was one of the most profound things I've ever experienced, and I haven't had a desire to drink ever since. That meeting really helped me see the power of the group and the power of what AA had to offer. I discovered that AA had what I had been looking for all of my life, which was unconditional love.

The past thirteen years of Molly's journey have not always been easy. With the support of AA, however, she has been able to remain clean and sober. "The beauty of this program," she says, "is that we all have our own journey, but we come together in these rooms, sharing our experiences. This program has brought me to where I am today." Today she is a successful teacher and recovering alcoholic.

Treasures of Strength and Weakness

And the wind said: May you be as strong as the oak, yet flexible as the birch; may you stand as tall as the redwood, live gracefully as the willow; and may you always bear fruit all your days on this earth.
— *Native American Prayer*

When I was a little girl, I went to the beach every summer with my family. It never failed that on the day before we left to return home, I could be found sitting on the shore with my sand bucket filled with water from the ocean. I wanted to take part of the ocean home with me. I wanted the ocean to be mine. I had it in my head that taking home the bucket of salty water gave me some sort of control over the ocean itself. I thought that taking seawater home with me meant that I wasn't really leaving; I didn't have to let go of it; it was mine. And each year I cried as my dad dragged me from the shore with an empty bucket in my hands.

Fifteen years have passed. My family no longer takes vacations to the beach. And I stand now on the same ocean shore of my childhood with a bucket full of seawater in my hands. I have found in the fifteen years since I last visited this place that the ocean is not the only thing that I wanted to control.

"Welcome to Southeast Recovery Center, Amanda. We're glad you're here," he said. "My name is Mark, and I am one of the primary counselors here. We are all here to help you understand and overcome your disease."

"What disease?" I snapped. "I don't have a problem."

"Amanda, you know as well as I do that you wouldn't be here if you didn't have a problem. Eating disorders are diseases just like alcoholism and drug addictions. Our responsibility is to help you understand and believe that, so that you can get better."

Even today I remember how angry I was at being put into the hospital for treatment. My eating disorder had reached the point that my therapist, Peggy, feared for my life. My physical appearance had been deteriorating for months as a result of my active anorexia and bulimia. I had lost a large percentage of my normal body weight, my skin was dry and gray, and my hair was falling out and leaving visible bald spots. Even more unsettling were the mental lapses that were becoming more and more frequent. At times I was so incoherent that I could not respond when spoken to, often forgot where I was going, and even ran red lights because I forgot what they meant.

"Amanda, you have a lot of people who care about you, but this program will not work without your cooperation," said Mark.

"I don't want to be here, and you know that," I replied. "I am supposed to be on a 445-mile bicycle trip from Maryville, Tennessee, to Savannah, Georgia. Instead, I'm in this hellhole with a bunch of alcoholics, drug addicts, and crazy people I don't know and with whom I have nothing in common."

"Well," he said, "I guess you'll just have to make the best of it. You're going to be here for a while. You have a choice—you can either be miserable, or you can try to get better. Group therapy starts in ten minutes, so I'll see you in there."

"Hi everybody," said Kim, the therapist who facilitated the group therapy sessions. "Amanda, since you're new, I want to explain that group therapy is a time when we share our experiences in recovery—both good and bad. The group is here to help you learn more about your disease and what you can do to get better. Let's go ahead and do introductions: tell us your name, your addiction, how you feel today, and whether or not you want to claim time to share."

On my first day of therapy, only four other people were in the group. I wanted nothing to do with any of them—they were all alcoholics or drug addicts and would never be able to understand what I was going through. I was not like those people, and I was stubbornly committed to separating myself from them. I intended to do the bare minimum while in treatment. I would do just enough to satisfy them until they would let me out. I didn't want to get rid of my eating disorder. It made life easier. I didn't have to worry about what I put into my body because I could immediately throw up. By the time I went into treatment, I didn't even have to force myself to throw up—my body naturally rejected anything I put into my stomach.

"Hi, my name is Diane, and I'm an alcoholic. I haven't had a drink in two months. I am feeling a little anxious today because I have to go to court tomorrow, but I don't want any time."

"Hi, my name is Jim. I am an alcoholic. I have been sober for thirty-five days now. I feel really good today, and I don't need any time."

"Hello, my name is Molly, and I am an alcoholic. I have three days of abstinence. I am very shaky from withdrawals, and I feel like shit. I'll take a little time today."

"Hi, my name is Vinnie, and I'm a drug addict. I've got a few things on my mind, and I will take some time. Oh, and I feel sad today."

"I'm Amanda. I have a problem with food. I feel terrible, and I don't want any time."

For the first few weeks of treatment, all of my sentences during "introductions" were short, choppy, and saturated with anger. I didn't even try to hide the fact that I did not want to be there. I constantly daydreamed about my bike trip and must have seemed like I was off in my own world. Sometimes, however, I couldn't help listening to the stories that the others told about their lives and their struggles with drugs and alcohol.

"Like I said earlier, my name is Vinnie, and I'm a drug addict. I am in this program because I am about to lose everything—my house, my children, and most important of all, my wife. I guess it all started when I was a kid. I was the oldest of four children, and my parents expected nothing less than excellence from me. I liked making good grades, and I worked really hard. I realize now that I did it for them, not for me. Even when I got married, everything had to be perfect. The stress became so bad that I turned to drugs. Drugs took me away from the demands of my family, my work, my life. I thought that drugs were the answer to all of my problems. It didn't take long before I started using entire paychecks to support my addiction. My wife had to buy all of the groceries, and we almost went bankrupt. I don't want to lose my family, but all I can think about is getting my hands on another line of cocaine."

I vividly remember Vinnie bursting into tears as he told his story. I had been terribly afraid of Vinnie when I began treatment.

He had tattoos all over his body and piercings from head to toe. Looks alone screamed that I was nothing like him. His story, however, was so similar to mine that I could not avoid experiencing a connection. He and I were both the oldest of four, victims of a relentless, foolish self-imposed perfectionism, and addicts because of a desire to escape the stresses of everyday life. While he attempted to control his problems using cocaine, I chose to regulate my life by controlling my food. But initially, I was too stubborn to admit the similarities between our stories.

* * *

"Amanda, we ask that you not purge while you are in treatment. That's one way of learning how to live without your addiction," explained Mark.

"Well, if I could do that, I wouldn't be here now, would I?"

Mark responded to my anger and sarcasm with the greatest ease and repose. "Still, we can't help you get better unless you are willing to work for it. We will do anything we can except do the work for you. You have to decide how badly you want to get better."

In actuality, I was not ready to get better. The thought of giving up my eating disorder, my comfort, my coping mechanism was extremely frightening. Even though the bald spots where my hair had fallen out were equally frightening, they did not provide me with enough motivation to stop purging.

"Hi, my name is Jim, and I'm an alcoholic. I have realized in the past few weeks something that has really helped me in my recovery. I have been drinking since I was in college. As I grew older and became a vital part of the company I was working for, the drinking only progressed. Eventually, I was suffering from severe health problems, but I refused to admit that they were related to alcohol. A few months ago, my wife caught me sneaking a drink after I had promised her that I had quit. She immediately walked out. At that moment, I realized two things. First I realized that I was losing a person I loved very much and was causing her to stop loving me; and second, I was killing myself. Finally, everything everybody had been telling me, everything that I had been denying, everything that I had ignored the existence of came as a stark, cold slap in the face. I was killing myself drinking, and I was going to lose everything that meant anything at all to me.

"Two days after that, I checked myself into the treatment center. At first I suffered from the 'I'm-not-like-them syndrome.' I never had a DUI. I never had a wreck. And I wasn't like those other people in treatment. It was a long time before I was able to look past the differences between the other addicts and me. When I finally accepted that I am an alcoholic, I was able to see that I am like them. I was finally able to begin learning from others who suffer from alcoholism. I'm glad to be here today, and I'm glad to be sober."

Listening to Jim, a light turned on. I could not get better unless I let people help me. I had to admit that I had a problem just like everyone else in those rooms. I had to admit that I could not fight this battle alone. The counselors at the hospital as well as my therapist had been trying for some time to make me understand what Jim had made clear in five minutes: I could not recover from my disease alone. I could not get better until I gave up some control.

Sitting on my bed that night, I contemplated the idea of giving this "recovery thing" a shot. The alcoholics and addicts convinced me that recovery is a long and treacherous journey. They made it clear during our sessions that recovery is always hard, never perfect, but a road worth taking. *Why,* I thought to myself, *would I want to do something so difficult?*

* * *

"This ride," explained Bruce, "could be one of the hardest things you'll ever do. We're going to be pedaling up and over mountains, across huge bridges, and through all kinds of weather conditions. We will ride in sun, rain, sleet, snow, and wind. I've been on

quite a few rides like this. As your trip leader, I promise that you will want to quit many times on this trip. Your body will hurt, your muscles will ache, and you will wonder why you are here. But I encourage you to keep pushing yourself. The ride will challenge you in ways that you never thought possible. When you finish this journey, you will have gained confidence, experience, and a tremendous sense of accomplishment."

✳ ✳ ✳

"Good morning, Amanda," said Kim. "You look a little tired; how did you sleep last night?"

"I didn't sleep much at all," I replied. "I was up thinking about some stuff."

"What kind of stuff? Do you want to talk about it?"

"I think I want to try this," I explained. "I think I'm going to try really hard not to throw up today."

"I'm glad to hear that. We're here to help you through it, so please tell someone on the staff if you need anything. It's not going to be easy, Amanda. I won't lie about that, but you can do this if you allow us to help you," she said.

I knew deep down that I had made progress, but my stubbornness and determination prevailed to a certain extent. I honestly wanted to try out this recovery thing. In my head I still believed that I could do everything on my own. I agreed to ask for help only to appease Kim. The events of that day, however, would actually begin penetrating my stubbornness, making me realize that I would, in fact, need help.

✳ ✳ ✳

"We will have a support van on this trip," explained Bruce. "It will be filled with water and Gatorade, granola bars, fruit bars, and other snacks to help replenish the fluids, electrolytes, and calories that you will burn while riding. Lisa will be driving the van. She will drive about ten miles ahead of the group and find a good stopping place. When you see the van, stop and get something to drink or eat. Then you can con-

⟞ 32 ⟝

tinue until you see her at the next ten-mile marker.

"It is very important that you stop and replenish your fluids. I also want you to eat a granola bar or something for energy at every two stops or so. Push your carbohydrates while we're riding. You'll be burning a lot of calories, and the food will help you maintain your strength.

"I realize that some of you are stubborn and will want to pass up the van and keep riding. I understand that it is hard to stop when you get into a rhythm. In spite of that, I really want you to stop. The van is there to help you, and it will support you through the duration of this trip."

* * *

"Amanda, are you ok?" asked Mark as he walked into the group room that afternoon. It was obvious when he walked in that I was going through the early stages of very unpleasant withdrawals. I was curled up in a fetal position on the couch clutching my stomach and struggling to hold back tears of pain. It was definitely one of my more vulnerable moments while in treatment.

"It hurts so badly," I cried. "I can't move. All I want to do is throw up, but I told Kim I wouldn't. My stomach hurts. My muscles ache. I don't think I can handle this! Please make it stop. Please! I don't want to do this. It hurts, Mark, please!"

"Amanda, you've got to breathe. Take some deep breaths. You can get through this. These are withdrawals. Your body is so trained to throw up that it doesn't know how to react when you don't. It will pass, I promise. Calm down and breathe. Think about something else."

"I can't, dammit! I can't breathe, Mark. It hurts. I can't think of anything else. Just make them stop," I pleaded.

"Just relax your body, Amanda. I know you have been in some of the groups where we discuss breathing techniques. Were you paying attention?"

"Yes," I snapped.

"Use those techniques that we have taught you. They will help you get through this. Lie on your back and take some deep breaths—in through your nose and out through your mouth. You can do this. Remember to fill your entire upper body with air and not just your chest."

"This isn't working, Mark!"

"You have to take more than two breaths, Amanda. Give it time. This isn't going to be a miraculous cure. Keep breathing, and the withdrawals will gradually decrease."

After what seemed an eternity but was probably only twenty or thirty minutes, the cramps, tension, and anxiety of my withdrawals had diminished. I was able to make it through group therapy that day, but I was utterly exhausted. Unfortunately, each meal brought on another round of withdrawals.

* * *

"WAKE UP, EVERYBODY!" shouted Bruce. "We've got a big day ahead of us, so I hope you all slept well. You'll definitely need that good night's sleep to get through today's ride. We will be riding up and over Newfound Gap, which is an eleven-mile climb straight up the side of the mountain. Anticipate your need to change gears so that your legs can adjust to the climb. You will all do just fine if you remember what I have told you about using the support van every chance that you get and focusing on something besides the pain. Most important, don't forget to breathe."

We pedaled through the cold rain for over an hour. I tried singing songs in my head and counting to 1,000, but it was hard to stay focused on something other than the pain in my legs. "How much further to the top?" I asked myself. "This eleven-mile climb seems like an eternity! Every time I think I'm close to the top, I round another curve, and it goes straight up again! I'm 'white-knuckling' it just to get up this rise. I keep thinking I'm just going to quit, but I won't. I guess I just have to hold on tight and get through this."

When we finally made it to the van, Lisa was very encouraging. "Keep pedal-

ing. You guys are doing great. This part is almost over. Here is some more water; make sure you are getting enough fluids. You have to take care of yourself."

* * *

"The beginning is always the hardest part of recovery," explained Mark. "You will do a lot of white-knuckling just to get through the bad moments. Withdrawals, anxiety, and exhaustion are inevitable stressors in the beginning stages of recovery. They are very tough to deal with, but you can get through them. Recovery means completely changing your lifestyle, but it takes a tremendous amount of work to get there. Most important is that you take extra special care of yourself as you begin your recovery program. The initial shock of recovery on both your body and your mind is overpowering and exhausting. Take care of yourself so that you can fight against your disease. Group is almost over, so let's end with the serenity prayer":

> God, grant me the serenity, to accept the things I cannot change, the courage to change the things I can, and the wisdom to know the difference,

said the group in unison to end that day's series of sessions.

I felt as if I was being tortured during the first part of recovery. Every meal was followed by at least half an hour in the fetal position crying because I wanted so badly to throw up. I simply hated the idea that there was food in my body. My world was a nightmare, but the people at the hospital continued to convince me that the hardest part would soon be over. I believed them only because I knew they had been through the same things that I was experiencing.

I spent a lot of time listening during this period, still refusing to talk during the group sessions. I became less bitter as the weeks passed, but I refused to smile and only spoke when I was addressed directly.

"Amanda, can I talk to you?" asked Lori as I walked out of the group room that day.

Lori was one of the few counselors during the first few weeks of treatment that I spoke to without being rude and sarcastic. I was afraid to let people near me, but somehow Lori was able to penetrate the wall I had put around myself.

"How many days has it been since you purged?" she asked.

"I guess it has been about five," I replied.

"Congratulations!" she exclaimed. "You almost smiled when you said that, too. How do you feel?"

"The withdrawals aren't as bad as they were, but they're still there. They suck," I responded.

"Yeah, they do, but at least they're not as bad." She stopped for a moment, looked at me, and said, "I'm really proud of you. Can I give you a hug?"

I hesitated only a second before moving forward and putting my arms tightly around Lori's neck. More than anything else, I felt very safe at that moment. I began to believe that the counselors were genuine when they said that they were there to help me. I had tried for three weeks to convince myself that they just wanted my money. Lori convinced me otherwise with a simple comment and a hug.

* * *

"Good afternoon, everybody," said Kim as she entered the group room. "Are we ready to get started?"

The day had already been strange because I was feeling a little better. I had eaten almost an entire piece of toast for breakfast that morning, and I had suffered from only minor withdrawals afterward. I was the last that day to do my introduction, and no one before me had claimed any time.

"Hi, my name is Amanda; I am anorexic and bulimic, and I feel fairly good today." There was an unusual silence in the room as I began to speak. I assume it was because I was talking more slowly and my tone had changed dramatically from the previous day. The bitterness and sarcasm seemed absent on this day, and I think that it caught the entire group, including the counselors, off guard. To everyone's surprise, I continued: "I think I would like to claim a little time today."

"All right, Amanda," began Kim, "it looks like you were the only one to claim time, so why don't you go ahead."

I had never been afraid to talk in front of people until I went into treatment. At that moment, I was so terrified of talking in front of the group that my eyes began to water and my hands started shaking. I had spent the entire night trying to plan what I would say if I claimed time, but now I could hardly make a sound. My fears were quite obvious because Kim immediately consoled me. "Take your time," she said. "We've got plenty of it."

"When I was in eighth grade," I began with a lot of hesitation in my voice, "each student in my health class went through a test to determine his or her body fat percentage. I remember being in the lower part of the normal range, but I quickly became obsessed with eating fat-free foods. I went home that day and told my mom that I couldn't eat anything with fat in it. I don't remember ever being concerned about body fat before that point. My mom is still angry about that because she blames all my self-esteem problems and my eating disorders on that incident."

I remember pausing for a few moments to determine whether or not I wanted to continue. My hands were still shaking from the anxiety of talking about my disease. A nod and a smile from Kim, however, told me that I needed to go on. From then on, the words seemed to flow from my mouth like water poured from a bucket.

"Anyway," I continued, "the next thing I remember regarding

anything with food didn't occur until I was in high school. During my sophomore year, my parents and I were really struggling to get along with each other. It was awful. My dad and I only spoke when we were being rude or screaming at each other, and my mom and I just couldn't seem to say anything nice about each other. After a while, the whole situation with my parents in combination with my belief that I had to make perfect grades and be a perfect volleyball player really stressed me out. To deal with the stress, I simply quit eating. I don't know why. I just chose not to eat so that I could get everything else done, I guess. I had a routine for meals. I would buy a slushie in the mornings at a local gas station to fill me up until lunch. Then I would eat a piece of bread with butter on it in the cafeteria, and that was it. I wouldn't eat anything else until the next morning's slushie because meals took up too much time.

"I don't remember ever thinking of it as an eating disorder. The whole situation seemed logical. I had things that I needed to do; so, I had to take out what I thought I didn't need. I thought that I could just live without food. Eventually, my volleyball coach convinced me that I needed to eat in order to play, and she made it clear that lack of nutrition was the reason for a decline in my athletic performance. So, I ate—heaven forbid something not be perfect in my life. After that, I started to eat more like a 'normal' person.

"This didn't last long, though. During my junior year, our high school softball team made it to the state tournament. I was taking batting practice for one of our first games, and I foul-tipped the ball into my face. My jaw was broken on both sides, but I was determined to play. So, that's what I did. I played the rest of my softball season and the following volleyball season with a broken jaw. All I could eat was baby food and soup. Almost eight months after the accident, I had surgery to repair my jaw. The surgery required that my mouth be wired shut and that I eat only from a syringe with a small tube on the end. I lost over ten pounds during the first week following my surgery. I guess from that point on, all I had to do to lose weight was refuse to eat. The best part was that I could always say that chewing made my jaw hurt too badly, and no one ever suspected that I had a problem.

"I graduated from high school and went on to college. I never consciously restricted my food until the summer before my sophomore year. At that point, I began to suffer severe stomach cramps every time I ate. To alleviate that problem, I just reduced my food intake. Because of my high activity level, I was able to drop lots of weight during that summer, and I loved it. When I returned to school and went back to playing volleyball, I didn't even try to change this pattern. I just wanted to lose as much weight as I could in the shortest amount of time.

"After a while, though, I got tired of restricting my food. I don't know exactly why, but I just wasn't getting the 'rush' that I used to get from starving myself. I would go for three or four days at a time eating nothing but fat-free rice cakes and drinking water, but it wasn't fun anymore. One night while I was babysitting, I finished off the strawberries that I had cut up for the little girl. In no time at all, I felt really sick to my stomach. Without a second thought, I walked into the bathroom, stuck my fingers down my throat, and threw up everything that I had eaten. I guess from that point on, I was hooked. I could eat, purge, and still control my weight.

"At first I only threw up when I was babysitting, which was once or twice a week. Eventually, I was eating little things like rice cakes and bagels just to throw up. Before I came into the hospital, I was purging thirteen or fourteen times a day. How I got into treatment is another long story, but I really don't want to talk about it anymore. I guess I'm finished."

"Amanda, you did a great job," said Kim. "I'm really glad you've opened up to the group. That's a huge first step toward getting better. It should get easier from here."

* * *

"I don't know if I can pedal anymore. These hills are killing me. I need a break," I whined as we climbed another steep incline.

The rest of the group was very encouraging. "You can do this: it will be downhill soon," they yelled.

I remember finally making it to the top of that hill near Cashiers, North Carolina. We were told that it was our last big hill of the day. We were exhausted by the time we reached the top. "Great job, guys. You have overcome one of the greatest hurdles of our trip," explained Bruce as we sat down for a short break and a bottle of water. "It takes a lot of willpower and determination to pedal up that hill into Cashiers. It should be a lot easier from now on. The rest of the day should be all downhill."

* * *

"Unfortunately," explained Mark, "nothing in life stays the same. It's always changing. It's never all downhill, but it's also never completely uphill either. I'm sure some of you wish that everything were really easy right now because you are going through some tough times. I'm sure you wish it were all downhill from here. You've taken the most difficult step, which is coming into treatment. Everything should be a breeze from now on, right? Wrong. Life doesn't work that way," he concluded. "All of you have to be on guard at all times for things that may trigger your disease and send you back into your addiction. This is something that will be with you for the rest of your lives. We will give you the tools, but you have to be willing to use them.

"I guess what I want you to get out of this session is that one of the most common reasons for relapse is complacency. If things are going well, you will start to think that you have conquered your disease. Life will seem to be an easy path. That's when life starts going uphill again. You will be bombarded from all sides by people, places, and things that will make you want to drink, or use, or purge. If you stop working your recovery program, you will relapse. I guarantee it.

I want you to know before it happens that life is always changing, and recovery is always changing. We are here to prepare you for those changes so that you can deal with them in a safe and healthy way instead of reverting to your addiction."

* * *

"This is crazy!" I shouted to Mary who was riding beside me. "I thought they said it was all downhill for the rest of the day. I swear that this hill is worse than the one up to Cashiers. I think that the drivers have gotten worse, too. I was almost hit by a pick-up truck back there! If nothing else, I guess it makes this ride more of an adventure," I said sarcastically.

* * *

"Are we ready to get started?" asked Kim as we all settled into our chairs to begin yet another group therapy session. It had been a few days since I had made my debut as a rational person in the group. I had been so exhausted from the entire experience that I could not do much more than sit and listen for the next few sessions.

"Hi, my name is Diane, and I'm an alcoholic. I just wanted to share that I have ninety days of recovery today. I know that ninety days is a very dangerous point in recovery, and that makes me really nervous. I have been having 'using dreams,' which is really scary. I wake up in the middle of the night thinking that I have relapsed because I was drinking in my dream. I don't want to go back to where I was. When I came into treatment, I was miserable. I embarrassed my children. I was about to lose my house because I bought liquor instead of paying the bills. My entire life revolved around alcohol. I am excited about making it this far, but I am also afraid of what lies ahead."

"Diane, would you like some feedback from the group?" asked Kim.

"Sure, I'll take some feedback if anyone has any."

"The way I see it," began Jim, "you're falling into one of those famous traps. It seems to me that you are worrying more about the future than about what is going on right now. They always tell us that taking things one day at a time is the only way to overcome our addictions. I would suggest that you focus on today. Tomorrow will come soon enough, and you can worry about that later."

"Thanks, Jim," replied Diane. "I guess I was getting so worked up that I lost sight of some of the most basic ideas of recovery. That was really helpful."

"Anyone else?" asked Kim. After a brief silence, she continued, "Molly, didn't you claim some time today? Why don't you go ahead and share."

"Well," began Molly, "I think I've been sober for a few weeks now, and the withdrawals aren't as bad as they were. It's so nice to be able to sit in a chair without shaking. Since my head has cleared up a little in the past week, I have been able to think about some things in a new way. I've met with my individual therapist about this, and she suggested that I talk about it here.

"When I was a kid and even a teenager, I remember my parents going through a lot of marital problems. For some reason, I was always caught in the middle of their stuff. My mom continually told me that my dad was a bad person and that she wished she could divorce him. My dad was always explaining to me that my mom was crazy and that she was the 'bad guy' in the situation. Whenever I lived through one of these ruthless blasts from one parent against the other, I would lock myself in my room and cry. I didn't want them to divorce, but I also didn't want to hear how miserable they were.

"One night, I called one of my best friends, crying about how much my parents hated each other and how I couldn't stand it any longer. She said that her parents were gone for a few days, and she invited me to come and stay with her. I assumed that she just wanted me to come over so that I wouldn't have to deal with my parents for a little while. When I got there, though, she had apparently raided her parents' liquor cabinet and had all sorts of drinks ready for us. I had never even tasted alcohol until that night. We drank together until the next morning, and I felt as if all of my problems were gone—at least for a little while. When I drank, I didn't have to worry about my parents. For a moment, their problems were not my problems. I loved it. I'm assuming you can all guess where I am going with this story.

"It wasn't very long before I was spending every night at my friend's house. We didn't drink her parents' liquor anymore, for fear that we would get caught. So we made some friends who were either old enough to buy alcohol or had fake IDs. Eventually, I thought about nothing but drinking. I dropped out of school during my junior year. I spent the next few years doing nothing but drinking. Because of my behavior after a big party one night, I ended up pregnant. I was so drunk all the time that I quickly lost the baby. I had serious complications when I lost the baby, and I was rushed to the emergency room. My blood-alcohol level was so high that the doctors immediately sent me up here for extended treatment. That's how I ended up in treatment.

"I guess I'm doing a little better, but I have a lot of resentment toward my parents right now. I feel like they have a lot to do with my alcoholism. I know I'm supposed to accept the choices that I made in order to take that first drink, but I just want to blame somebody else."

Molly's eyes filled with tears. She stopped at that point because she just could not deal with everything—her parents, the drinking, the lost baby. She buried her face in her hands and refused to look up for a few brief moments. Each time she tried to say something, she would break into tears.

"Molly," said Kim, "you don't have to finish right now. You've done really well to share as much as you have today. Dealing with feelings that you have suppressed is very difficult, but it is a vital part of recovery. It is actually one of the best parts and one of the worst parts. When you stop drinking, purging, or using, you have to start dealing with the feelings that your addiction helped cover up. Once you deal with those feelings, though, you will feel a huge weight lifted off your shoulders. Recovery is a long process."

To everyone's surprise, including my own, I looked up and asked, "Can I say something?"

"Of course you can," Kim replied.

"Well," I began, "it is scary how much Molly's story sounds like my own. Please don't get me wrong; I love both of my parents so much, but they have put me through some shit during my life. I always seemed to end up in the middle of all their problems. My mom and dad were always using me as a sounding board while venting their frustrations about the other. I think that one of the main reasons I started restricting my food was so that I had control over something. I obviously had no power over my parents; so I was just looking for something to control.

The momentum of my comments carried further. "Then, I went off to college where I thought I would be separated from my parents' problems. Somehow, I still often found myself between their problems. College brought other challenges that added to my need for control. I constantly felt pressure from my friends to look better and to dress nicer for my boyfriend. I guess I took their suggestions to the extreme, and that's when I became conscious of wanting to lose weight. I became obsessed with controlling my figure, which I achieved by starving myself or purging." Suddenly aware that I had opened new doors and gone further than I had intended, I stopped abruptly as I finished that sentence.

I had heard the counselors say over and over again that people often turn to drugs, alcohol, or food to cover up feelings or emotions that arise as a result of the chaos in their lives, and chaos is a way of defining the need for control. I finally understood and comprehended this idea of control that had been repeated and explained in so many treatment sessions. It took Molly's story for the idea to hit home. I could relate to her story, and it all started to make sense.

"Amanda, you got quiet all of the sudden; are you ok?" asked Kim.

"Yes," I replied. "I was just thinking; I'm finished talking."

"I think you've realized something very important today, Amanda. It's very clear that you love your parents and your friends, but they have put you in some unfair situations. You have spent years holding in and covering up the anger, frustrations, and resentment toward them. Within these rooms you can start uncovering and dealing with those feelings, and I think that you have started that by speaking up today. It is very important that you continue to uncover all of those feelings that you've kept hidden for so long."

"It's gonna suck, isn't it?" I asked.

"You have been through a lot of pain to get where you are now, Amanda, and I won't deny that you'll have to go through some more pain in order to get better. That's why we're here, to support you and help you as you begin to uncover all of those feelings. It will be even harder for you because you have built up many layers to protect yourself from various situations. You are going to have to force yourself to let your guard down and be vulnerable. I know that sounds terrifying. But as you peel off those layers, we will teach you to replace them with healthy things like support groups and prayer.

"All right," she continued, "our time is up. Let's end with the serenity prayer."

"God," we began in unison, "grant me the serenity to accept the things I cannot change, the courage to change the things I can, and the wisdom to know the difference. Amen."

As I began to leave the group room that day, I felt a tap on my shoulder. I turned around to see Diane motioning me to come back in so that she could talk to me in private. Although I found this a little strange at first, this moment marked the beginning of a special friendship.

"Amanda," she began, "I just want you to know how nice it is to see you happier. I know things aren't great, but you seem to be coming up out of a bad funk. I'm really glad that you're here. I also wanted to give you something, if that's ok."

"Sure, I guess," I replied with a tone of obvious skepticism in my voice.

"Don't worry," she assured me, "it's nothing bad. I just wanted to give you my ninety-day recovery chip. Hopefully it will remind you that you can do this if you work at it. What's that thing we say at the end of sessions? You know, it works if you work it, but you've gotta work it every day. Don't forget that. I just wanted you to have a little reminder until you get your own chip. Keep talking in group; it helps a lot."

I could not hold back the smile that swept over my face. I flung my arms around Diane's neck and gave her a huge hug. I really didn't want to let go. More than anything, I was seeing that I had so much in common with these people. I could learn from them if I would allow myself to be taught. I had spent many years building a wall around myself so that no one could get close to me. It was going to take a lot of work to break down that wall and truly open up to these people. For so long everyone around me had believed that my life was great and that everything in my life was fine. I had made such an effort to look good to everyone else that I had convinced myself that things were great—despite the fact that I was purging many times a day. I had covered everything up for so long that it was going to take a lot of work to uncover the real Amanda. Hugging Diane, though, made me realize that I had made yet another step in my recovery. I was slowly starting to peel away the layers that covered the true me.

After group that day and in the days that followed, Diane and I spent many hours talking, sharing, seeking, and proposing answers. Our friendship quickly blossomed, and we were soon acting as if we had known each other for many years. The twenty-year difference in our ages never seemed to matter. She shared with me the wisdom of one who had spent the previous ten years in various treatment centers searching for the strength and motivation to live a life without alcohol. Her insight came from years of learning lessons the hard way. I valued every second Diane was willing to spend with a young, scared, college student suffering from a disease she barely understood and against which she had fought for half her life.

✳ ✳ ✳

"Good morning, everybody! I hope you all slept well. We've got another big day ahead of us. We will be riding from Anderson to Saluda, which is about a 75-mile ride. Most important, I want to warn you that even though this is South Carolina, it's freezing outside. Please put on as many layers of clothes as you can. Wear your fleece jackets, extra shirts, extra socks, and ear warmers if you have them. I'm not lying. It's really cold out there. It's going to hurt until your body gets used to it or you go numb—whichever comes first. Let's just hope that you don't go numb."

"How many layers do you have on, Amanda?" asked Mary. "I have on so many that I look like the Stay-Puff Marshmallow Man! I can't believe the temperature has dropped so much overnight."

"Actually, I'm afraid that I'm going to freeze all day long unless the temperature goes up," I replied. "Do you have any extra clothes that I can borrow?"

"You can borrow my fleece vest if you want. I think I've got on clothes that will keep me pretty warm. Do you want it?"

"That would be great," I said as she handed me the vest. I put the vest on, and we headed out the door to our bikes. The chill in the morning air was shocking. Even though I knew it was going to be cold outside, my body was taken by surprise when I stepped out of the heated room where we had spent the night.

"Oh, my goodness!" I shouted, slowly adjusting to the cold. And, of course, things got worse as the ride began. "My legs aren't cooperating this morning. I'm having a hard time pedaling."

"You're not the only one struggling, Amanda," said Bruce. "We're going a lot slower than yesterday. That cold air can really throw off your rhythm."

"What rhythm? I can't pedal long enough to even establish a rhythm," I replied, trying to milk some humor from the situation. "This is almost as bad as riding up an eleven-mile incline. In fact, I don't know which is worse."

We rode approximately ten miles before taking our first rest stop. By that point, my fingers were frozen and purple. I had thought that my body heat from pedaling would warm me up, but it was just too cold outside. Before pedaling on, I put on another jacket that I had borrowed from Lisa, and someone else loaned me a pair of gloves. Riding a bicycle with four layers of clothing on was quite difficult, and I had very little control over my body because of those layers.

As the hours ticked away, and we put more and more miles behind us, the sun slowly began to peer out from behind the clouds. "Hey, there's the van," I yelled.

"Good job, everybody!" shouted Lisa as we rode into the next rest area. "Are you warming up any at all?"

"I'm doing a little better," I replied. "I think I'm going to leave this big jacket in the van for the next part of the ride and see how I do."

"Here, I'll take it for you," said Lisa as she reached out to help me take it off before adding, "It will probably be easier to ride without this big jacket on."

"I hope so. I was struggling," I called over my shoulder as I rode off. "See you in ten miles!"

As the day wore on, the sun got brighter and the temperature gradually increased. At each rest stop, I found myself peeling off more and more layers of clothing. I quickly got rid of the fleece vest, then the ear warmers, and then the long-sleeved shirt I was wearing. I was left in a sleeveless T-shirt and my bike pants, which covered my padded bike shorts.

"I think I'm ready to leave these pants in the van," I said as I came to a skidding halt next to the van and quickly dismounted from my bike. "It's really getting warm out here. It feels so much better than it did this morning. Here are my pants, Lisa. Will you put them in the van for me?" I asked.

"Sure, no problem. You look like a totally different person without all those clothes covering every inch of your body! See you in ten miles or so. Have fun."

"Oh, wait!" I yelled as I turned around and sprinted back to the van. "I forgot to get something out of the back pocket of my pants."

"What is it?" asked Lisa with a puzzled look.

I hesitated for a moment before explaining to Lisa about the chip. "Actually," I admitted, "a friend of mine is recovering from alcoholism, and she gave me her nine-ty-day recovery chip. I brought it with me to remind me not to quit even when this ride gets really tough."

"That's really awesome." she replied approvingly. "Have fun. I'll see you in a lit-tle while."

As I pedaled the last ten miles of that's day's ride, a bright sun beat down on my shoulders and kept me comfortably warm. So much had changed since we rode out of Anderson, South Carolina, that morning. The temperature had risen almost forty degrees. I had peeled off at least four layers of clothing, and my disposition had changed from miserable to spirited.

"I'm so proud of you guys for pushing through the cold weather this morning. It would have been really easy to quit under the circumstances, but you pushed yourselves and worked hard to achieve your goal."

✿ ✿ ✿

I went to group therapy feeling as if I had betrayed my parents and my friends. My guilty conscience had taken over. I was afraid that I had made them seem like bad people, which was far from the truth. I went into the group that day determined to amend everyone's views of my parents and my friends. I asked for some time during introductions and waited anxiously for my turn.

"First of all," I began, "I want you all to know that I feel terrible for what I said about my parents and my friends yesterday in group. I'm not denying that they did those things, but they are not bad people. In fact, I owe my life to my friends for getting me into treatment. My best friend is the one who confronted me about my eating disorder. She was so worried that she spent a lot of her sophomore year trying to find people who could help me. She practically saved my life by convincing me that I needed to go into treatment. I guess I just feel bad for putting some of the blame on other people. That's all. I just wanted to clarify what I had said yesterday."

"Does anyone have any feedback for Amanda?" asked Kim.

"I do," said Jim. "It seems so obvious, but it's hard to understand when you are in the middle of it. People are going to make mistakes, Amanda. They're human; we all are. That doesn't mean that you can't still love them with all your heart. That's why we are taught to forgive. Your parents made some mistakes. They put you in some awkward situations. It was wrong. Now you can learn from their mistakes and help them learn from those mistakes, too. You are allowed to be angry both with your parents and your friends, but you must also realize that they are human beings. Unfortunately, things like that are going to happen for the rest of your life. You are in here to learn a healthy way to deal with those situations."

"Thanks, Jim," I responded.

"Anyone else?" asked Kim.

"I have one more thing to say," added Diane. "I learned in a group once that I don't have to apologize for my feelings. I think that is what Amanda has done today. She felt guilty about being angry. If nothing else, I have learned that it is perfectly acceptable to feel angry, sad, upset, disappointed, or any other feeling. The important thing is to feel the feeling and deal with it—in a healthy way. Don't hold it in, and don't hurt yourself by drinking, using, or purging. This understanding has been really helpful to me in dealing with all of the things that have happened since I began my recovery. Maybe it will help you, too," she concluded.

"You've gotten some great feedback today, Amanda," said Kim. "I hope that you will take everything in and try to use what everyone has told you. They've said the same things that I would have told you in this situation; I guess they *have* learned something in here," she added with a slight grin. "It's almost time to go, so let's end with the serenity prayer."

* * *

"This session is going to be a continuation of one we had last week," explained Mark. "I told you last week that one of the main causes of relapse is complacency. The cravings and withdrawals will become less severe, the road easier, but there will be other obstacles to overcome. These obstacles will usually come unexpectedly, so you must always be prepared to deal with them. Things like the death of a family member, the loss of a job, or an unexpected situation will often make you want to go back into your disease. It's a matter of learned habit to turn to your addiction for comfort. It is so important at those moments that you be ready to use the tools we give you in treatment, so that you can fight the temptation to use.

"One of the most important things we will ever teach you in treatment is to establish and rely on a support group. Addicts, especially those with eating disorders, have this idea that they can do everything by themselves. Amanda, you and I have talked about trying to do everything without asking for help. Do you mind sharing some of that with the group?"

"No, I don't mind," I responded. At that point I had been in treatment for almost six weeks. My attitude toward recovery had changed dramatically since I had first entered the hospital. I had become more willing to talk during group sessions, and I was even learning to give both constructive feedback and suggestions to help others who were beginning a recovery program.

"When I came into treatment," I began, "I refused to ask for or accept help from anyone. I thought that I could do everything all by myself. On the one hand, I was a control freak, and I was convinced that nobody could do anything up to my standards. In other words, I was too damn stubborn for my own good. On the other hand, I was so afraid of burdening others with my problems that I refused to ask for help. I didn't feel as if my problems were worthy of asking for help: I didn't have cancer; I hadn't lost a loved one. So, I thought that my problems didn't deserve any attention. I've learned in treatment that I must be willing to ask for help. It's the only way that I'm going to get better. I first had to accept the fact that I have a disease, just like cancer or diabetes. Just like those patients, I need help to get through my disease. Whether I needed someone to sit with me after a meal or someone to answer a simple question, I knew I could rely on the support of the people here. My support group has even extended to include people I have met in some of the evening meetings that I attend. Most important for me, though, is to include my higher power in my support group. If I can't get in touch with someone when I'm in a tough position or struggling with my recovery, I can always turn to God. I have found a great deal of comfort in knowing that God is always there for me. Still, I don't always turn to God first, and that's a part of my recovery that I am working on. I guess that's it. I've got a lot of work to do on my recovery, but at least I'm working."

"Thanks for sharing, Amanda," said Mark. "A strong support group is vital in recovery. I want to leave you all with a picture that I hope will remind you of the importance of a support group."

At this point, Mark held up a beautiful painting of a flock of geese. The geese were in perfect formation except for three geese on the right side. One of the geese was apparently too tired to continue; the two other geese were flying underneath to keep the first from falling. "Geese actually do this," Mark explained. "They fly in formation to block the wind for those behind them, but they will break that formation to keep one of the group from falling. This, in my opinion, is the ultimate support group. Just remember that the next time you see a flock of geese."

* * *

"Today is our longest ride," began Bruce. "We will ride a total of ninety miles before this day is over. But it's also our flattest ride. We're out of the mountains now, so you won't have to worry about any major climbs. We may try to send the van fifteen miles ahead instead of ten so that you can maintain a good rhythm. Is that ok with everyone?"

"YEAH!" we shouted in unison. "Let's go!"

We started our ride that day fully aware of its length. We knew that by the end of the day we would be exhausted simply because of the length of the ride. When we set out that morning, the group separated as usual. Road bikes are naturally faster bikes than mountain bikes or hybrids, so road bikers typically wait until those on slower bikes get a head start of several minutes. Eventually, they pass the larger group and arrive first at the next rest stop, but the time differential is relatively small. Before long our people on mountain bikes were spread out behind the road bikers, and one of the group leaders brought up the end. By the end of the day, however, unexpected obstacles would actually bring us together into one group.

"Hey, Mary, can you believe this wind?" I shouted. "It's awful. I feel like it's hitting me from all sides! This wasn't in the weather forecast was it?"

"I don't know about that, but it's killing me. I can't decide if it's hitting me in the face or from the side or all of the above! I thought today was supposed to be easy."

"I've got an idea," I yelled to her over the gusts of wind. We'll do a mini-pace line. I'll ride directly in front of you and block the wind for a while. When I get tired, you can take over. Think that will work?"

"It'll be hard with only two people, but we can give it a shot," she replied.

We rode the next ten miles in this mini-pace line; for a while I blocked the wind for Mary, and then she did the same for me. When we rode into the next rest stop, we talked to the others who were riding mountain bikes. We explained how riding together in a pace line blocked the wind and made the ride a little more tolerable. They agreed to give the idea a try, and the five of us began the next section of our ride as a unit. With winds up to twenty miles per hour still attacking us, our little group pressed on, each front wheel only inches behind the rear wheel of the rider ahead, and actually found a consistent rhythm by the time we reached the next rest stop. For most of the day our little pace line pulled us along the flat but windy South Carolina highway. Rest stop after rest stop, we chopped into the appointed ninety miles.

"We've got about twelve miles left today," said Bruce after we had gotten water and a snack. "You have all done an excellent job—especially with that wind. It was an obstacle I never anticipated. You are all exhausted, and these last miles will be trying. Rely on each other and work together to make it easier. Let's get going."

Without any further instructions, we lined up to begin the last twelve miles of our ride, but the formation was different from what it had been for the previous 350 miles. Those with mountain bikes didn't leave ahead of those with road bikes. Instead, we all rode together. The road bikers spread out among the mountain bikers in the pace line. We fought, pedaled, and pulled each other for twelve straight miles against the battering wind, refusing to be blown to a stop. We fought as a group, we pedaled as a group, and we reached Allendale, South Carolina, late that evening as a group.

* * *

"Hi gang," said Lori as she walked into the group room that afternoon.

"Are you working with us today?" I asked hopefully.

"I am," she answered with a smile. I saw Lori only on those rare occasions when she filled in for someone or did a special group with us. For some reason, I had connected with Lori from the beginning of treatment, and her presence was always special for me. She had a way of getting through to me when no one else could. But she also didn't let me get away with anything. I remember her telling me once, "I love you very much, but I'll call you on your shit." She always knew what it took to get through to me, and I have always been thankful for that. During this session with Lori I received a piece of advice that has kept me from falling back into unhealthy patterns on more than one occasion.

"Today," began Lori, "we're going to look at situations and characteristics that encourage addictions, and then we'll talk about some of the steps you can take to avoid relapse. Things such as DEPRESSION," she said as she wrote the word on the board, "and IMPATIENCE can lead to addictions. What are some other characteristics that lead to addictions? Let's start with you, Molly. Can you give me an example?"

"I think for me it would have to be feeling worthless. I was always made fun of when I was a kid. I was the awkward kid with glasses, and my dad was the principal of my school. The other kids were ruthless toward me, and it's difficult to deal with that when you're young. I think those feelings carried over into my adulthood. I drank because I thought it made me 'cool' and made me part of the popular group. I suppose I also used alcohol to escape those feelings of worthlessness. When I drank, I didn't have to think about all of the things people might say about me."

"You've made some really good points, Molly," said Lori as she wrote the word WORTHLESSNESS up on the board. "What about you, Jim?"

"I just wanted to be socially acceptable. In my circle of friends you weren't socially acceptable unless you drank. So I became socially acceptable—I drank."

"That's a good one, too. Diane?"

"I don't know," said Diane. "I really don't feel like talking today," Diane said. "Can you go on to someone else?"

"I can, but are you all right?" asked Lori.

"I guess I just don't feel very well," replied Diane. As I look back, I remember that there was something very strange about Diane that day. I know that everyone has a bad day from time to time, but she seemed very distant. Her attention span was non-existent, and she wouldn't acknowledge us when we tried to make her feel better. Still, I assumed that it was one of those days when she simply wanted to be left alone. So, that's what I did. I left her alone.

"That brings us to you, Amanda. Can you give me a characteristic?" she asked.

"I have learned in treatment that I have the most common type of personality for developing an eating disorder. More than anything else, I am the type of person who imagines that she can and must do everything exactly right. I want everything I do and everything I have a role in to be perfect. If it's not up to my standards, then I'll do it again. I've always put a lot of pressure on myself to be the best. It isn't that I'm better than anyone else; it's that I am terrified of failure. That's just the way I am. Even after being in treatment for a while, I don't understand what's so terrible about that. I just like things to be done well. Is that so wrong?" I asked.

"It's not wrong, Amanda," answered Lori, "but you need to learn the concept of moderation. We've talked a few times about your work-load and all of the things that you do. I know as well as you do that you are an overachiever. She stopped momentarily to collect her thoughts. Then she continued, "If you learn nothing else from me, promise me that you'll remember this . . ."

"OK," I agreed.

"Allow yourself to be human, Amanda." A puzzled look must have immediately swept over my face because Lori quickly continued. "You can't do everything. I have heard you talk about studying for hours a day, working out for three hours a day, babysitting until crazy hours of the morning, and countless other things. I don't know if there are enough hours in the day to do all the things that you do and stay healthy."

"I don't think I do that much, Lori. I play ball and go to school."

"And you baby-sit for two or three days at a time, too, right?" she asked.

"Well, yeah, but I've got to make money."

"And you lift weights, run, and ride your bike for extra exercise in addition to regular practices, right?"

"Yeah, but that goes along with volleyball." I answered.

"Do you hear yourself, Amanda? Do you realize what you're saying?"

"Yes," I answered.

"Do you think that you are rationalizing everything, trying to find ways of excusing what could be a dangerous habit of living?" she asked.

I thought long and hard before answering her question. I knew perfectly well that I was rationalizing the situation, but I didn't want to admit it. I knew very well that I had been trying to take care of too many things. I also knew that my extreme perfectionism was one of the major factors leading to my eating disorder. Still, I hated to admit that she was right. I was afraid of slowing down. I was afraid of grades below an A, weight gain, and a lack of money. In my eyes, I had to keep going to avoid my worst fears.

"Amanda?" she repeated as the group awaited my response.

"I really don't know," I finally answered.

"Why don't you think about it tonight, and you can discuss it in group tomorrow. Believe it or not, we've used up almost all of our time, so we'll finish this topic later. You guys can have a fifteen-minute break before your next session." As usual, we ended with the serenity prayer and walked out into the hall for our break. As Lori walked out, she motioned me over to talk one-on-one.

"How are you feeling?" she asked. "You seemed a little shaken up when I confronted you."

"It's because I know you're right," I admitted. "I'm afraid to slow down, and you know that."

"I'm going to tell you the same thing I said in there—allow yourself to be human. It will be okay. You will be okay. In fact, you'll be a lot healthier if you slow down and take time to care for yourself." I wasn't sure how to respond, so I gave her a hug and told her that I would think about it. Before she left though, I asked her one more question.

"I'm graduating from the program on Friday," I began. "I know that Friday is your day off, but I was really hoping that you would come if you're not busy."

I could tell from her facial expression that she was busy on Friday, but I waited patiently for her answer. "I'm supposed to be out of town on Friday, but I will come if something changes," she answered. I remember being terribly disappointed. I wanted her to be there so badly because she had been such an important part of my treatment. Still, she gave me hope that something might change, so I tried not to dwell on it too much. I spent the rest of the day in my room trying to figure out exactly how I was supposed to "allow myself to be human."

* * *

"Seventy miles to go, gang!" shouted Bruce as we gathered our bikes. "The weather isn't looking too good today, so be ready for anything. We hope to make it to Savannah around six o'clock, but the weatherman said to expect high-speed winds from a storm off the coast. Keep your eyes on the sky. If we get separated, make good decisions. Use each other. Ride in pace lines to block the wind and be especially careful on the slick roads when cars are passing. Have fun, and we'll stop in about fifteen miles to see how everyone's doing."

I rode away that day expecting the rough winds but confident that I could deal with them. Five of us established a pace line early in the morning and were able to maintain a decent speed despite the wind. The weatherman had predicted the conditions accurately for the last day of our ride. In addition to the wind, we rode through rain, hail, and fog for the first forty miles of the day. Still, our group was on a roll. We had established a steady cadence and a fast speed. Then the unexpected happened, and my situation changed dramatically.

"SHIT! SHIT! OH MY GOSH!" I screamed as my front tire brushed Leah's back tire. Before I could brake or swerve, I went flying over my handlebars into a ditch. I landed directly on my head and popped my neck. My legs were cut up, and my face was covered with dirt and grass. For a few minutes, I could do nothing but lie motionless on the ground. There were bikes everywhere, and the entire group was crowded around me. They were asking the typical questions: "Do you know where you are?" and "What day is it?" to make sure that I was coherent. I knew that I hadn't broken any bones, but I was hurt.

Nothing, however, was going to stop me from going the last thirty miles of our trip. Eventually, I stood up, dusted myself off, and looked at my bike. The handlebars were slightly bent and my chain was broken, but nothing seemed more serious. So, we wrestled with my handlebars until they were straight enough to ride, and we replaced the chain. Once again, we were on the road with eight miles to go until we reached the van.

I had to struggle to get going again, to keep up, because I was hurting and my rhythm was non-existent. My face and legs were cut, bruised, and bleeding, and my neck was stiff. It took every ounce of energy I had to keep up with the group. Each turn of the pedals left me more frustrated than the last. I had to finish the trip, but I wasn't sure if I was physically able. By the time we finally reached the van, I was in tears. My body ached, but I tried to hide the pain from everyone. As I sat on the curb, Bruce came over and joined me.

"How are you feeling, kid?"

"I'm fine," I lied.

"How about putting your bike on the trailer and riding in the van for a few miles. I think a break would do you good. What do you think?"

"Please don't make me do that," I pleaded on the verge of sobbing. "I want to ride the entire way. I don't want to wimp out."

"Amanda, you're hurt. It's perfectly fine to take a break. No one is going to look down on you for taking care of yourself and resting."

"But I really want to finish, Bruce. This is so unfair," I said angrily.

"We'll be here for a few more minutes. Think about it and let me know."

I have always sensed a dramatic difference between what I need to do and what I want to do. I knew as well as Bruce that I needed to be in the van for at least the next ten miles of our trip, but I was too stubborn to give in to the pain. 'Amanda, allow yourself to be human.' What would people think if I stopped riding for a little while and took a break? Would they think that I was a coward or would they respect my decision? 'Amanda, allow yourself to be human.' Many different thoughts ran through my head during the last few minutes of our break. Although it took a while, I realized that the best thing for me would be to take a *break. I had already ridden over 415 miles; I wouldn't prove anything by riding the last thirty miles in agony.*

"It's your call, Amanda. What's the plan?" he asked.

"Here's the bike. I'm gonna ride with Lisa for a little while," I answered.

"Good decision. You don't have to do it all," he finished with a smile. "I'm proud of you."

I was extremely disappointed when I got into the van, but I cannot deny that it was nice to rest. My muscles were completely exhausted, and I had developed a terrible headache from the wreck. We drove to the next rest area to wait for the group to arrive. Lisa and I knew we had at least an hour to waste because the winds would inhibit the bikers from riding as fast as usual. While waiting, we talked and laughed and got to know each other much better. We found that we had a lot in common, and it wasn't long before we were acting like long-time friends.

"You know," I said, "I would never have gotten to know you if I hadn't wrecked. I guess something good came out of my being forced to take a break. Now I'm actually sort of thankful it happened."

"I know," she responded. "It's been nice to have someone to talk to while I wait. Hey, is that them coming?"

"It looks like it. Do you want me to help you get the food and drinks ready?" I asked.

"That would be great," she answered. "Go get the Gatorade, and I'll get the granola bars."

As the first group rode in, it was clear that something was wrong with Drew. Without a word or a smile, he passed Lisa and me and dismounted his bike. He immediately began putting his bike on the trailer as if he was not going to finish the ride. I couldn't help overhearing the conversation that took place as Bruce went over to talk to him.

"It's just too hard," Drew explained. "I don't want to do it anymore."

"Are you sure, Drew," asked Bruce.

"I don't want to fight the wind and rain anymore," he explained.

"Drew, please don't take this the wrong way, but are you going to quit every time something difficult hits you? I mean, life isn't always easy. I realize that this is only a bike ride, but I don't want you to quit just because it's hard. You knew it would be tough when you started. This is your choice. I know you may not realize this now, but there may come a time in your life when you might regret not having pushed yourself to find out what you are truly capable of doing. This is your opportunity to find out just how tough you are and how much you can endure."

"I don't care," he snapped.

"You are doing really well, Drew, but it's your decision. I wish you would reconsider," Bruce said.

"I don't want to," Drew replied with an air of finality in his voice. He walked toward the van and got in without speaking to anyone. He seemed almost angry, but I didn't dare approach him. He seemed intent on being left alone. So, that's what I did. I left him alone.

* * *

"Is everyone here," asked Kim.

"Diane isn't here yet," I answered.

"We've got a lot to talk about," said Kim, obviously avoiding my statement. I knew that she had heard me, so I scanned the room to see if anyone else had noticed. I could tell by the puzzled looks on the faces of all of my friends that they had noticed Kim's unusual avoidance of my statement. For a moment, I was angry with Kim. As I stared at her in disbelief, however, my attitude quickly changed when I noticed a small tear moving down her cheek. I assume everyone else noticed as well because the room was completely silent.

Finally, Kim began, "I've got some bad news for you guys. I've been given permission to tell you this, so I want you to know that I'm not breaking confidentiality. I wanted to tell you during our group session today so that you could talk about it if you need to." Kim stopped momentarily as if waiting for our permission to continue. Instead, she looked into a sea of completely confused and apprehensive faces. My mind was racing with a variety of scenarios. Nothing, however, could prepare me for what she revealed next.

"I hate to be the one to tell you this, but Diane was found dead this morning in her room," she explained, obviously fighting back the tears. "Most of you know that she had advanced cirrhosis of the liver; the doctors believe that she died of complications from that."

A sense of shock swept over the room. We had all known the previous day that something was wrong, but we never expected this. "This is going to be difficult to deal with, but I want you all to know that we are here to help you through the grieving process. The hardest part is probably going to be dealing with the fact that Diane had finally chosen recovery, but her disease still won. We all know that she was a wonderful person who was working a strong program. Unfortunately, her alcoholism was too advanced when she decided to come into treatment. We have no control over that."

"This isn't fair," began Jim through his tears. "She was ready to live and then this happens. It just doesn't make any sense."

"Well," answered Kim, "it's hard to accept, and it's not fair. Unfortunately, some of it does make sense. The choices we make have consequences. She spent many years of her life drinking. It reached the point that her body simply couldn't fight anymore."

The group continued for a long time. We cried, we hugged, and we did our best to support each other in the midst of this tragic news. We were given a lot of information regarding the grief process. I don't think that Kim or Mark actually expected us to remember much of it at that moment, but they were required to educate us for safety purposes. I do remember, however, their emphasizing that it takes a lot of time to overcome, to live with the loss of a good friend. They reiterated how important it would be to work our recovery program so that this loss did not send any of us into relapse. They made it clear that we were all in that danger.

We were encouraged to ask for the support that we needed to get through this crisis. I chose to spend a great deal of time alone in my room. To deal with Diane's death, I cried, prayed, and wrote in my journal in order to work through the variety of feelings that over-whelmed me. Only one day after Diane's death, I found myself in the midst of yet another storm.

"How are you this morning, Amanda?" asked Kim.

"I've been better," I answered completely exhausted from a night of crying.

"I know it's hard, but you can get through this. I came to see you because we found something as we were going through Diane's things. This envelope has your name on it. I guess she never got the chance to give it to you."

I took the envelope from her but was afraid to open it. Kim left to give me some privacy, but she asked that I come and get her if I needed anything. I sat there for a long time wondering what Diane might have written in this letter. We had grown very close during our time together in treatment. Outside of the group sessions, Diane and I spent a lot of time with each other. My final conversation with Diane echoed through my mind before I gained enough courage to break the seal of the letter. She had said to me:

> Amanda, you have so much ahead of you. I look at you and realize that I have missed out on so much. I never went to college; I never flew in an airplane; I've never even seen the ocean. But I have a good feeling about you, kid. Not every-one can fight an addiction. We both know how hard it is, but you have the strength to do it. Promise me that you won't forget that.

"I promise," I replied. Then I read her letter.

> My Dearest Amanda, Some people on this earth have what I call inner strength. These people are gifted with the ability to make it through the storms of life and still find

the time to touch others in the process. You, my friend, are one of those people. Although our paths crossed under extreme circumstances, my life is better because of your friendship.

I cannot imagine the pain that you are experiencing right now, and for that, I am eternally sorry. While I see so much strength within you, I do not have that strength within myself. I am old and tired, and the road was too hard for me. It does not have to be that way for you, Amanda. You are young, talented, and full of life. Move on, my dear friend. Achieve great things, make good choices, and touch many more lives in the process. I have no doubt that you will. All my love until our paths cross again. —Diane.

My mind was racing as I finished the letter. All at once I was looking reality directly in the face. Did Diane really die of natural causes? Was Kim protecting our group from something? What had really happened to Diane on the previous night? Questions overwhelmed me. Answers evaded me. There was only one thing that was clear—the addiction won.

I wanted to be angry with Diane for leaving me. I wanted to feel guilty because I thought that maybe I could have stopped her. I wanted to be sad because I had lost a dear friend. I felt all of those feelings and none of them at the same time. With no tears left to cry, I lay silently on my bed. Eventually, I succumbed to exhaustion, closed my eyes and was sound asleep.

I could see Diane's face so clearly in my mind. It was the only picture that I had of her. We looked at one another for a long time before she broke the silence. *Don't forget what I've told you, kid. All of the power that you need is within you. You also have God, your family, and a great support group. I'll always be here, too,* she added. *All you have to do is close your eyes, and I'll be there. I promise.*

"Don't go!" I shouted as she turned to walk away. "Don't go, don't go," I cried.

"Wake up, Amanda, wake up," said Lori as she gently tapped my shoulder. "Were you having a bad dream," she asked as I opened my eyes.

"It was about Diane," I admitted.

"I know it's hard. We're all sad, but we can get through this together. Eventually, you'll find that you can let her go. Don't get me wrong, she will always be in your heart. If you work through this, though, you'll find that gradually you can let go of all the pain that you feel right now. You cannot change what has happened, but you can focus on your recovery and not allow the same thing to happen to you."

"I know, but it's hard to stay focused on anything right now."

"Just take it day by day or even minute by minute if you have to. What have we taught you in here?"

"One day at a time," I responded automatically.

"Well, we've at least taught you the idea," she said with a grin. "Now you have to put it into practice."

"Yeah, I guess you're right." She looked at me intently with her you-know-I'm-right look. I grinned and raised my eyebrows to show her that I got the point. After a brief staring contest, I gave in. "I know you're right," I admitted. "Thanks for staying with me for a little while."

"You're welcome. I want you to go spend some time with the others. I think it will be good for you. Don't stay up too late. You have a big day tomorrow."

"OK," I agreed. And then I added, "I hope you'll be able to come."

* * *

"Only ten miles to go, everybody! We should be in Savannah in an hour or so. How are you feeling, Amanda? Are you ready to get back out there?"

"You'd better believe it!" I said as I put on my helmet and gloves.

"What about you, Drew?" he continued.

"No," Drew sharply answered and turned to continue sulking in the back seat of the van.

"Well, that's your choice." After a brief pause, Bruce shouted, "Well, what are we waiting for? Let's get going!"

* * *

"We have a lot to accomplish today, so we need to get started," began Kim. "I think that this is one of the biggest turnouts that we've had for a graduation in a long time. We have three people graduating today, and I'm going to let them decide who wants to go first."

Jim, Molly, and I looked at each other. This was a big moment for all of us. It was also a scary moment. I was thrilled about finally making it to this point in treatment. At the same time, I was terrified about leaving both the security of the hospital and the people I had met there. I was going to delay the inevitable as long as I could. Molly agreed to graduate first.

Mark continued the opening remarks to the gathering, arranged around the room in a great circle. "The graduation of our patients is a very special ceremony," he explained. "They have worked very hard during their time here, and we send them out with reminders of what they have learned in treatment. We do this with a card. Printed on this card is our phone number, the serenity prayer, and a list of positive affirmations." Mark grinned as he began the next part of his explanation. Those of us who had been in treatment for a while had witnessed quite a few graduations, and we anticipated the corny line that was coming: "This card is laminated with a magic coating. As we send this card around our circle, each person will hold the card and silently put whatever blessings he or she wants into the card. The magic lamination makes all of the blessings stick," he added with an extra grin for those of us who were snickering. "We ask each graduate to choose two people from all of us assembled here, who will sit on either side of him or her. One will start the blessings card and pass it around the circle. Obviously, the last person will finish the blessings card and give it to the person graduating. So, Molly, go ahead and choose your two people, and we'll get started."

"I want Amanda to start my card and Kim to finish it," she answered. I was totally surprised by Molly's choices. In my opinion, being chosen means that you have made a difference in that person's life. I was already emotional, but I was almost in tears as I began her card. I held it tightly in my hands while looking her straight in the eyes. I silently prayed for God to give her the strength she would need to go back out into the world. I sent her blessings of peace and acceptance. As I handed the card to Ray, who was sitting next to me, I noticed the door begin to open. Into the room walked the two people who had been more instrumental than any others in leading me toward treatment. Peggy, my counselor, and Cydna, a close friend, had persuaded me to enter treatment despite my skepticism and stubbornness. At first I had entered treatment to appease the two of them, but it had developed into one of the most positive experiences of my life. They joined the circle, and I could not stop smiling. This was my opportunity to show them that I had made progress, and I owed much of that progress to them.

Molly's card continued its silent passage around the room. The circle was larger than usual because of all the family and friends who had come to the graduation. Molly's parents and her boyfriend were there, Jim's entire family had come, and Cydna and Peggy were there for me. Even Vinnie, who had graduated from our group a few weeks earlier, returned to see us. Molly's card eventually reached Kim, who held it for a few moments, handed it to Molly, then stood up and hugged her for a long time. When the clapping had ceased, Molly was given the opportunity to say a few closing words in front of the group.

"I never thought I would actually want to live," she began. "When I came into treatment, I was uncooperative, depressed, and suicidal. I hated the world. It's not been an easy couple of months, but I can honestly say that I feel much better."

Molly finished talking abruptly and went over to her parents and boyfriend. She sobbed as her parents held her tightly in their arms. I remember being thrilled for Molly at that moment. Her parents were making an effort to understand her disease simply by being there. Watching them, however, also filled me with sadness because my parents were not. I was afraid that my parents would not accept my disease, so I chose to leave them out of my recovery. I also could not handle the thought of hurting them. At that moment, however, it sunk in that, just like Molly, I could forgive my parents and myself for all of the mistakes we had made in our relationships. I finally knew what it felt like to need my mom and dad more than anyone else.

Apparently, I had been deep in thought because I suddenly felt Molly nudging me with Jim's card. He had chosen his two companions, and the card had already made its way to me. I took the card, looked him straight in the eyes, and silently prayed before passing the card to Vinnie. I looked up a few moments later as the door opened once again. Lori quickly found a seat so as not to disturb the ceremony. She had made it, and I thanked her with a huge smile and a wave as soon as we made eye contact. She acknowledged me with a nod and a smile that said, "You knew I wouldn't miss it." The day was almost complete. My only regret was that I had not invited my parents.

* * *

"Hey Mary, does that sign say what I think it says?" I yelled.

"I can't see that far," she yelled back.

"Savannah City Limit! Savannah City Limit!" I shouted as we rode closer to the sign. "We did it! Can you believe that? This is awesome!"

Some of the group had already reached the sign, and they had stopped at the van, parked next to the sign on the side of the road. It was not long before the rest of the group arrived. Bruce wanted to get a picture of all of us at the sign so that we would have something to serve as a visual reminder. A few people asked Drew if he wanted to be in the picture, but he just mumbled something and turned away. He seemed to be trying to disconnect from the group entirely.

"You have all worked very hard, and I want you to have something to remind you of this trip," Bruce began. "It's been quite a journey," he continued. "I can't speak for everyone, but I have had a great time. I hope that this trip will give you an idea of the great things you can accomplish—not just in bike riding, but in all different aspects of your lives. Not everyone can complete a trip like this, but you have persevered through lots of tough stuff and made it to this point. I'm very proud of you, and I want you all to be proud of yourselves. Congratulations, gang, and welcome to Savannah!"

Although our group was small, our shouts were almost overpowering as Bruce finished his comments. People in cars waved and honked as they passed our group. Although they may have been laughing at us, I like to think that our group had some-how made a positive impression on them. We glowed with pride and excitement. We may have been on the side of the road, but it was our moment to shine, and we savored every second of it.

✳ ✳ ✳

"All right, Miss Amanda, it's all yours. Who would you like to start and end your card?"

Without hesitation, I answered, "I want Peggy to start it and Cydna to finish it." They moved to either side of me as Mark handed Peggy my card. As she looked at me and sent blessings into the card, my eyes filled with tears once again. I was so happy, yet so scared; I was so proud, yet so nervous. More than anything, I was feeling over-whelmed by the entire experience until the door opened once again and interrupted my thoughts.

I only saw her profile as she walked into the room. She was a taller, thinner version of me with dark, black hair and dressed in a stylish, summer business suit. The man who entered behind her was a tall, handsome gentleman dressed in his worn-out khaki shorts and his favorite navy-blue shirt. I stared in disbelief. I did not know why or how, but my parents had made it just in time to join my graduation ceremony. From that moment on, the tears streamed. They were unstoppable, and the use of tissues was futile.

My blessings card continued around the circle. Lori glowed with pride as she filled the card with her blessings. The fact that she did not have to come made it more meaningful and unforgettable. Before long the card reached my mother. She gripped it in her hands as she read it, closed her eyes, and kissed it before passing it on to my dad. As he read the card, I could see the tears beginning to form. The power in that circle was overwhelming, and the blessings from everyone flowed over me before I even received the card. My dad looked up and winked at me, which released a single tear down the side of his cheek. He never wiped it off; he simply passed the card to the next person.

When Cydna was finally given the card, she put her arm around me before filling it with her prayers. As she handed me the card, she gave my hand an extra squeeze and said, "I am so proud of you. Enjoy this."

"Do you want to say anything, Amanda?" asked Mark.

"I'm sort of embarrassed because I'm crying," I began. "For those of you who don't know, I hate to cry, and I've done it more in the past few days than I've done in years." I took a few seconds to compose myself before trying to finish. "Like Molly, I hated life when I came into this program. Since coming in, I've made many dear friends, and I've even lost a dear friend. I've learned more about myself in the past seven weeks than some people learn in a lifetime, and that's scary," I added with a grin. "More than anything, I'm just thankful to be alive. Life didn't look too promising when I first entered treatment. So many times I've been the comic relief in these

rooms, and it's difficult for me to stand up here and be totally serious. So I'm going to stop before I ruin this moment. I really appre-
ciate all of you. Thanks."

After the ceremony my friends and everyone in treatment bombarded me with hugs and congratulations. All of the counselors made
sure to give me a few extra words of reassurance before leaving: Peggy
gave me a card and a new journal; Cydna slipped a small note of
encouragement into my hand before going. I had been in treatment for
what seemed a lifetime, but it was over in an instant. I quickly found
myself picking up all of my things and slowly walking toward my parents who were standing in the opposite corner of the room. The three
of us stood in silence. Soon they stretched out their arms, and I found
myself sobbing once more. "It's all going to be fine, Panda," began my
dad. "We want you to tell us what you need us to do. We love you,
and you don't have to go through any more of this without us."

"But . . . how did . . .how did you know?" I stuttered.

"Well," began my mom with a bit of hesitation in her voice, "we
got a strange phone call last week from a lady who said that you were
graduating. She didn't tell us much, but she made it clear that we needed to be here. I think her name," she paused a moment to recall, "was
Diane."

* * *

Several years have passed since I left the safety and security of treatment. I walked through the doors that day prepared to face the world
and all of its many challenges. I was confident that I had the tools, the
support, and even a guardian angel to help me face the various torna-
does of life. I learned quickly, however, that having the tools and using
the tools are two entirely different concepts. While in treatment I had
learned a variety of methods to avoid a return to my disease. After
ninety days of abstinence, however, I chose not to use those tools, and
I relapsed. Within the first few years after leaving treatment, I relapsed

multiple times, and I faced a variety of other losses and setbacks. Each obstacle, however, was accompanied by a new lesson, and each setback provided a new path on my journey toward recovery.

Today I look into the vast expanse of the ocean, filled with count- less ambiguities, dangers, and opportunities. Yet, I am no longer afraid of it. I no longer have to be in control of it. Letting go of control is not defeat; letting go of control is a way of dealing with the torna- does of life head on—bending without breaking, like a willow in the wind—and of learning to find shelter and support in the fury of a storm. Looking out at the ocean, I understand that the journey is never over. Just like the waves, life is always changing, and the journey never ends. Peacefully, I place Diane's recovery chip in my bucket full of this year's ocean water, pour the water back into the ocean, and walk away directly into the wind.

Acknowledgments

I have a story—one of adversity, friendship, support, and triumph, a story that almost ended abruptly four years ago. It is because of the following people that my story continues, and I take this opportunity to thank them all for their love, wisdom, guidance, and support.

First and always foremost, I thank the good Lord above for having a plan. Though I may not always agree with or understand that plan, I trust that it is right.

To my dear friend Melanie, thank you for your willingness to risk our friendship to save my life. You truly are a brave soul, and I thank God each day for allowing our paths to cross.

To Cydna and Peggy, thank you for putting up with me, standing beside me, and refusing to give up on me. The two of you have worked hand in hand over the years to bring me back from a very scary place. Words cannot describe the special place you hold in my heart. I love you forever.

I owe special thanks to Lori Martin and Mark Smith for helping turn an angry, scared, and tormented girl into an outspoken, confident, and happy young woman. Along with the rest of the EHRC team—Kim, Ray, Mary, Cheryl, and Jim—you worked your magic and gave me back my life. Thanks to you I am alive.

I am so appreciative to Linda Clark for the constancy of her belief in the promise of this project. At times it seemed like "Mission Impossible," but we always found a way to overcome the obstacles.

After three years and thousands of miles, we can finally see the fruits of our efforts. Thank you for sharing your knowledge of life, your friendship, and your command of the written word.

To my special friends at Wesley Woods, may God bless you for defining true friendship and teaching me the importance of having a solid relationship with God. Thursday nights at the Campfire Circle will forever remain one of my favorite memories. David, Deanna, Charlie, Carol B., Christy, Gary, Sarah Cav, Kim, JR, Lucas, Joy, Tasha, Erica, Shellie, Kasey, Micah, and everyone who was on the summer staff from 1998 to 2000—never stop working to change the lives of everyone around you!

To my Bike Savannah crew from MC, thanks for all the support. Without knowing it, you made this project possible. I especially want to thank Bruce, Mary, Lisa (Momma Hen), and Cathy for encouraging me to "keep going" when I thought I could go no further. Keep pedaling!

To Leah and Lindsay, thanks for your never-ending love and support. Your friendship has helped me through countless trials and tribulations. I love you both and wish you the best.

To Coach Schram and the 1997–2001 MC Volleyball teams, thank you for your examples of discipline and love. Girls, we had some good times! Four years of blood, sweat, and tears, and we always managed to laugh. Thanks for taking me back for my senior year and allowing me to have the greatest season of my life.

To Missy, Mary Jo, Debbie H., John and Gail, Debbie R. (wherever you are), Marcia S., and Beth, thanks for leading the way and even pulling me along by my fingernails at times. You are the soldiers who clear the path and lead the rest of us in the right direction.

To Ruth Ann Laneman, Theresa Parker, the Best families, the Moore family, the Hinchee family, the Harris family, Dr. Schneibel, Dr. Klingensmith (a.k.a. Dr. Dan), Dr. Berry, Dr. Craig, Dr. Cowan, Dr. Soud, Dave Powell, Laura McCullough, Sharon Wood, Olivia

Blair, Sandra and Benny P'Pool, Skip Savage, Linda Moore, Kay Garrison, Paul and Rebekkah Longmire, Erin Russell McCarty, Chad and Erinn Luke, Shannon Aird, Vinnie and Julie Vineyard, Kathy Rankin, Bob Baker, Jill Riley, Penny Dotson, Christy Gregory, Jeanne Hartman, all of my volleyball girls from Junior Olympics and Maryville High School, thanks so much for the support, tears, laughter, and hugs. I love you all.

To Bard and Sherrye Young, thank you for putting this book together. The chance of meeting people as talented as you while riding my bike across Tennessee was so remote—it's uncanny. It proves to me that some things are meant to be. Thanks for everything.

And last, but never least, to my family both near and far, I have put you through so much in my short time on this earth, but you stood beside me through it all. Dad, Mom, Aaron, Eric, and Emily— you are my foundation. My grandparents, aunts, uncles, and cousins are the reinforcements. I am never alone. I love you.